WE ARE FUTURE

WE

ARE FUTURE

LADISLAUS BOROS

HERDER AND HERDER

1970
HERDER AND HERDER NEW YORK
232 Madison Avenue, New York, N.Y. 10016

Original edition: *Wir Sind Zukunft,* Mainz,
Matthias-Grünewald-Verlag, 1969.
Translated by W. J. O'Hara.

Nihil obstat: Brendan W. Lawlor, Censor Librorum
Imprimatur: Robert F. Joyce, Bishop of Burlington
June 20, 1970

CONTENTS

CONTENTS

Introduction

This book was not written for philosophical or theological purposes. It is a series of meditations on hope. In a meditation, intellectual effort and prayerful concentration merge; it is impossible to say exactly where one begins and the other ends. A person meditating is not out to prove anything, only to express direct experience in the simplest possible language, seeking to realize that God is present, and to make it possible for others to do so too. Often enough it would be hard to say whether that presence means delight or terror, or both. Meditation is an attempt, as Luther himself pointed out, to get to grips with some fundamental experience in the life of the believer, wrestling with it by diligent attention and reflection on what the Holy Spirit means by it.

What we should like to achieve, therefore, is a deeper awareness of the divine and human mystery of our hope, in a spirit of prayerful concern with this mystery. Christian life is a fruit of hope. It is essentially prospective, forward-looking, a departure into the unknown, an exodus. It is concerned with what is still open, still to come in life. Christ has gone before us into the mystery of an absolute future. Consequently, to wait in hope is the native element of a Christian's life, experience, thought, and prayer, the fundamental personal attitude in which alone he can

7

glimpse the real meaning of his faith. Jürgen Moltmann exactly describes this feature of Christian life when he says that hope is not just one item in Christian life, but is the absolutely indispensable condition for actually engaging in that life. The "God of hope" (Rom. 15, 13) is the immanent *logos,* the very soul of the life of faith, and therefore orientates and gives purpose to our prayerful reflection on our relations with God.

The original message of the new covenant was the announcement that in Christ a completely new dimension of reality had opened out, that of heaven. "From that time Jesus began to preach, saying, 'Repent, for the kingdom of heaven is at hand' " (Mt. 4, 17). It is also the mystery of history that heaven is growing and coming to maturity around us and in us, in the children of God, in the brothers and sisters of Jesus Christ. Since that time it has not been possible to understand man on the merely factual basis that he exists here on earth. His life is directed towards heaven, towards a condition that is at hand yet still to come. The fact that heaven is at once close and distant creates an intermediate zone of tension and strain, a domain of freedom to obey or disobey, hope or resign. All that happens before heaven, all the seeking and groping that constitutes a large part of the history of mankind and of each one of us, is only a coming to birth. The world only fully attains existence when man enters heaven. We are not yet alive in the real sense. We do not yet see, hear, or understand the essential. The human reality we possess is essentially incomplete and to come. Consequently, reflection on a concrete existential theology of hope involves no less than the task of envisaging in relation to heaven the dynamism which is inherent in all created reality and in all Christian thought and prayer.

A Christian who has felt the breath of hope remains restless,

inquiring and seeking, whatever momentary and superficial satis-
factions he may experience, tinged as they are for him with sadness. At the same time, he knows that the fate of the world has
already been decided by Christ's resurrection. As we consciously
or unconsciously live as Christians, that is to say, in Christ, we
are infallibly moving towards heaven. In the temporary and provisional, the final and definitive fullness of the promise is already
operative. No quest ends in the void. This certainty gives serenity and joy to Christian life. Nothing can separate us from
the love of Christ (cf. Rom. 8, 35-39). Once and for all we have
to come out into the open, free and gay. "I have set before you
an open door, which no one is able to shut" (Rev. 3, 8). In a
world of promise and hope such as this, there is no reason for
the Christian to be faint-hearted.

The word "God" will occur frequently in these theological
meditations. It is a word that means little or nothing to many
people nowadays. Despite that fact, or, rather, precisely because
of it, we must use it here, placing it in front of us again in its
radiant clarity and simplicity, and acting upon it once more in
the actual details of living. If any reader of this book cannot
believe in God any more, we will say quite simply, with Karl
Rahner, that if and as long as they cannot, as honest human
beings, make an act of faith, they should not and may not do
so. Anyone who honestly and in conscience thinks he cannot
manage to do more than stand helplessly confronted with *mystery,* as a "troubled atheist," or who despairingly sees and feels
nothing but the absurdity of his own life, should quietly admit
this to himself and even attempt to accept this experience itself
as in a profound sense grace. God will turn even that into a
blessing for him, the believer must admit. Anyone who feels
bound by his responsible and honest obligation to the truth (in

order to remain true to conscience) to stand helpless in face of many questions—even apparently in face of ultimate questions—and leave them open and unanswered with all the strength of his mind may, can, and must do so. He is even under an obligation to do so. Before God, who is supremely magnanimous and reserved, he can attain his eternal salvation only in this way.

For us Christians, however, it is a case of treating people of this kind in a friendly and courteous way, after God's example. Christianity is not a collection or inventory of truths, all of which have to be held or adopted with equal urgency in order to be in the "unity of truth." Christianity is more like an opening in the reality of the world which leads from innumerable partial truths, and even errors, into *the* truth. But this one truth of Christianity is in fact God's incomprehensibility. The Christian will not "find" his God anywhere. What he says, therefore, is only true if it is speech that leads to silence in the face of mystery, leaving the mystery in its mystery, not replacing it by a word or concept. This is the spirit in which we wish to speak about God in this book.

The sequence of ideas in these meditations is as follows. At beginning and end are two meditations in which theoretical effort predominates (Outline of Hope; Future of Hope). These serve as frame for reflections which take some idea outlined at the beginning and develop it in increasing detail to its ultimate consequences. The first meditation may perhaps demand a certain effort from some readers. If so, they can start with the second and take up the first again later. Perhaps, however, on a careful reading the contrary may prove to be the case. It is often easier to cope with thoughts and ideas than with something that demands commitment of our whole self and life.

It is not the business of a collection of theological meditations to list what they have consciously or unconsciously derived from others. Of course the author has many friends and kindred spirits to thank for what he has learned from their talk and writings. In any case, our meditations on hope will have to omit many important problems. Inquiry into mystery inevitably has a history, and the Christian above all need have no hesitation in leaving some questions alone. He humbly (modestly but courageously) recognizes himself to be incapable and incompetent, in the confident trust that all human failure is encompassed by the mercy of God.

1

An Outline of Hope

"What no eye has seen, nor ear heard, nor the heart of man conceived, what God has prepared for those who love him" (1 Cor. 2, 9). This text is fundamental for hope, and must stand as promise, warning, and pointer at the very start of our meditations. We must certainly let the eternal fulfillment of all our desires, heaven, emerge as it were from the totality of our earthly experience, but at the same time we have to project earthly longing above and beyond what is humanly attainable. That is the only way we can make valid statements about heaven. Heaven is something that totally and utterly transcends our powers, but it is also something that it is impossible for us not to desire.

Bearing this in mind, we should like primarily in this first meditation to allow our purely human aspirations to find expression, and to form some idea of heaven as the point where our human impulses and emotions converge and are fulfilled but transcended. What bases of supernatural fulfillment are there in human reality? In other words, we are looking for adumbrations of heaven in earthly life. But before beginning our actual reflections, we must first consider the question of principle, in order to explain how man can glimpse the invisible, catch some echo of the inaudible, and form however distant a conception of the transcendent.

The Dynamism of Human Existence

Man is chiefly aware of himself as dynamism, as driven from within outwards, as longing and hope, desire and striving, restlessness and disquiet, furious competition and unsatisfied nostalgia. In all kinds of ways his own existence shows him that reality is inherently dynamic. He also observes something similar in the external world, especially in the tenacious and inexhaustible thrust of evolution. In our world, what has been attained is nowhere sufficient. In man, however, the "cosmic spearhead" of evolution, the immense longing of the universe for what is new and promising, concentrates and culminates. In our own vital impulses and emotions we experience in an intense form the world's yearning for creative invention. We bear within us the mighty dynamism of the world, the very force which impels its evolution and drives it to ever higher stages of development. To form some idea of the world's longing, of the inherent dynamism of reality, all we have to do (but this is indispensable) is to become quite still and listen attentively to the depths of our own being. This attentiveness to what is within is also the very first condition for gaining some earthly knowledge of heaven.

The source of our own longing and of the dynamism of the universe is hidden from us. The origin of these tendencies can never be brought fully to light. Clearly the dynamism of our existence is an ineluctable destiny. Man can never escape it. He is driven by it even against his own will. Even to escape from it would be an expression of the same drive. The very will to

14

do nothing is still a will; even self-destruction is an action. But we have no direct intellectual access to this inescapable impelling element in ourselves. The root dynamism of our personality is stirred to life before anything has been done. The very thought that seeks to grasp it is an expression of it, and this shows that something ultimate and decisive is involved. Now whenever something ultimate and decisive is in question, it ought to be thought about prayerfully, in meditation. Our thought has to feel its way forward to that innermost limit where our being is held in God's hand and disappears beyond our ken. This is a second radical presupposition of the considerations that follow.

Though our inherent dynamism tells us nothing of its origin, it nevertheless makes known its goal. It unfolds into numerous, quite often incompatible tendencies. At the same time, it becomes evident that there is incompatibility and tension not only between the various different tendencies but also within the intrinsic structure of each. Every human aspiration springs from contraries, is dialectical in character. Each particular impulse is an unstable balance of opposites. The latter indicate the direction of the essential dynamism. Accordingly, investigation of the inner opposition of the impulses can render explicit what is tacitly implied in the radical dynamism of our existence. Such an inquiry calls for what we might term a concrete mode of thought. We have to evoke the subject of inquiry from our own personal experience of life, discover the marks it has left in our own individual life history. Consequently, to think about heaven here on earth always constitutes a particular, personal endeavor. That is the third presupposition of our reflections.

Every moment of heaven will constitute a perfect balance of opposites, sublimating their antitheses and soaring above the abyss of Yes and No which constitutes our being. Human exist-

15

ence in its pure intensity will be realized in heaven. If, therefore, on the basis of our experience we can adumbrate an inner balance of human tendencies and illuminate the rare moments of equilibrium in our life by reference to their eternal pattern, we shall comprehend something of the scale on which supernatural fulfillment will expand our small, restricted earthly life.

It is necessary to adopt this laborious method of elucidating the concrete and particular, for without actual representations, our finite minds feel lost in a void of nothingness. We must decipher the language of the unimaginable in representations and symbols. A final proviso, however. Philosophical insight is never the kind of knowledge that we can simply possess. The individual himself has to discover his certainties for himself. He cannot coerce himself into finding them. Philosophizing can only confirm what each has already found out by experience. It can give encouragement and protection against vacuous, incompetent thinking. It can throw light on the quiet power of anticipation, to which the consciousness of infinite fulfillment will correspond.

A World Transparent to God

A first pointer to the state of eternal fulfillment is to be found in the inner tension of human self-giving, devotion, love.

Self-Fulfillment as Fulfillment of the World

Human consciousness attains its own identity and actuality only through the presence of what is other than itself. The world is, therefore, not merely a condition of the possibility of human personal life; much more radically, it is the fundamental universal determining feature of man's finite reality, a basic characteristic which all the rest presuppose. What is other is always the first datum in the activity of the human being. The individual ego is always merely consequent. This shows how fundamentally and irreparably man is immanent in the world.

This structure of conscious activity exhibits a general law of human existence. Man only becomes man by losing himself in what is other than himself. Being human essentially consists in self-giving. To lose oneself is to find oneself; surrender leads to self-possession. An embodied mind or spirit is therefore intrinsically and necessarily bound up with the world. Man's implication in the world is not something that a finite person engages in in addition to his existence as a spirit; it is a necessary factor in his actual activity as spirit. Spiritual assimilation of what is other than the self is a condition of the possibility of self-awareness. As we have already indicated, self-realization takes place by self-giving. The fundamental form of all human aspiration or endeavor is, therefore, that of attentive and receptive preoccupation with another, an affectionate dwelling on what is given to us, a selfless and self-effacing presence for a being other than oneself.

This certainly does not mean that people cannot destroy or suppress this fundamental attitude of aspiration or endeavor. Like other gifts, selflessness makes demands and can develop into a virtue only in a few lives of achieved perfection. That is why really unselfish people are so few and far between. As Hugo von Hofmannsthal says, that is why people who can listen quietly and attentively are esteemed as rarities. A genuine reader is just as rare. Rarest of all is someone who allows his fellow men to influence him without incessantly disturbing and even destroying this influence by his inner restlessness, vanity, and egotism. In

17

essence, it remains true that man is derivative and dependent. He can only enter into himself by going out from himself, only find himself by seeking and accepting what is other than himself. The essential can therefore only be received in an attitude of self-giving which seeks no advantage or special interest but is one of sheer devotion, that is, love. Love is therefore the real application of the mind to reality, for it alone draws the true consequences from what is other than the self. Consequently we cannot ourselves achieve even our own fulfillment; it is given to us in response to our self-giving.

Refusal on principle to give oneself to what is other is therefore self-stultifying. C. S. Lewis expresses this fundamental fact as follows. Love makes us vulnerable. If we love something, our heart will certainly suffer and quite probably be broken. The only way to be sure of keeping one's heart from harm is never to give it away, not even to a pet animal; to surround it with fads, avoid all entanglements, shut it away safely in a coffin of egotism, where safe, dark, still, airless, it will fall to dust. There is only the choice between tragedy, or the risk of tragedy, and self-damnation. The only place outside heaven where we can be perfectly safe from the danger and grief of love is hell. To go out towards reality is, therefore, an essential element in man's self-realization.

We are already in a position to draw a first conclusion for our thinking about heaven. It is clear from what has been said that any fulfillment of our humanity can only be thought of as at the same time the fulfillment of the world, because this is a condition of our own transformation. Our reflection on the dynamism of human self-giving discloses an inescapable community of destiny between man and the world.

18

Self-Giving: *Aspiration to the Absolute*

Without wishing (or being able) to call in question the truth of what has been said so far, we must nevertheless complete it dialectically by a negation. For the human spirit to give itself to a finite being presupposes that it is already tending above and beyond the finite towards what is unlimited, ultimate, and unconditional. Our immanence in the world is itself rooted in our transcendence of the world. The whole movement of self-giving is only possible and intelligible if it already implies an anticipatory reaching out towards the one, absolute, and infinite Being. In giving himself, man is seeking an unconditional beyond all that is conditioned, an infinite beyond all that is finite. This is the fundamental reason why man essentially transcends the world.

Since love is the highest form of human self-giving, it can therefore throw light on what has been said. First of all, in love we have the joyous confirmation that we belong to this world. In the love of a human partner our self unfolds. Even the world opens out for us, for our very involvement in the world is transformed by love, even what is closest and most familiar to us. We experience many things as though for the first time; the old takes on a new significance, the present appears in a fresh light, and the future assumes new promise. Yet precisely in this confirmation that we belong to the world a new demand that love makes on us becomes clear. We must go beyond, transcend the person we love, and have indeed already done so by the fact that we do love them. By inherent necessity our love carries us beyond the form that it actually assumes. It is less the actual appearance of the beloved that we love than the mystery he or she is. That

19

is why love seems so strangely out of proportion to its object.

We might refer to the poets. They break out of the world of experience in their search for terms of comparison. In their ecstasy they have recourse to contradictions, to everything in the universe, flowers and animals, clouds, stars and oceans, in order to describe the beloved and the world radiant with their love. We are never weary of the person we love and the world in which they live, because we love them and as long as we love them. Quite often other people cannot understand how this is possible, cannot see anything special about the person in question (though they may say nothing of the sort for the sake of the lover). Parents know by experience exactly the same thing. In the face of a child there is something that ultimately only the eye of a father or mother can see. That is why a love that has come to full maturity is always reticent. It is an essential characteristic of a beloved person to be unfathomable, as limitless and full of mysteries as the universe.

Consequently, the beloved introduces the lover into a transcendent domain. He realizes that the lover loves in him more than he really is; that as beloved his reality consists essentially in being a preliminary, in introducing something more that transcends him. After the beloved has awakened love by his presence and drawn it to himself and become all in all for the lover, he must become transparent, cease to be, so that love may flow to the object for which it had always really been meant. This is what constitutes the nobility of the beloved, of love, and of the lover. It is said that the eagle cannot take flight from flat ground but has to hop awkwardly onto a rock or tree trunk; then he can soar to the skies.

Consequently, self-giving is never brought to completion except by an inner separation, an aspiration to the absolute. This detachment achieves the most precious transfiguration of self-giving, which is reserve. This alone confirms the seriousness of the self-giving and at the same time opens out the transcendence behind the form of the beloved. Thus human love itself is always an anticipatory aspiration towards the absolute totality of reality, and at the same time, even if only unconsciously and implicitly, it is a reaching out towards the infinite being of God. Transcendence of the world is therefore an essential feature of created spirit and is always intrinsically involved in its endeavor to give itself in love.

A second conclusion follows from this. Heaven can only offer human fulfillment through sharing in God. Man's ontological situation in heaven, so to speak, must be God himself. Or, as Augustine puts it in the *Enarrationes in Psalmos,* God himself is our locus after this life.

The Transparency of the World to God

On the basis of the polarity we have just described in human self-giving (immanence in the world and transcendence of the world), we can now form some idea of the state in which these two contraries are not suppressed but remain on a higher level of being, interwoven in indissoluble unity. Sometimes even in earthly life a somewhat similar unity and sublimation is realized. "A lover will understand what I am talking about." On occasion, transcendence may assume the face of a beloved person and become immanent in the world. God mysteriously shines forth in a finite person. Then the latter is no longer a way to transcendence but the ultimate goal of our dedication. The created has become a vessel of the divine. Earthly reality is pervaded by a definitive reality. The creature, vulnerable, threatened, and essentially transi-

21

tory, forms for a moment the content of our aspiration towards the infinite. More divined than perceived, a diaphany takes place—God shines through in the creature or the world becomes transparent to God. Love of God, affection for a creature, and earthly devotion coincide in such moments of highest earthly fufillment, without, however, ceasing to be distinct.

It is this interweaving of divine and created which alone makes a pure (wholly disinterested) love of God possible and at the same time inescapable. Wherever we turn, we find God as the outcome, content, basis, and goal of our own inclination. Furthermore, it is the case that in these moments the love itself is no longer really our own doing. It is God who is loving himself in us and through us. Man attains here that intensity of being to which he has been called from all eternity. He becomes a self-expression and self-representation of God.

Now if we project into an everlasting condition what is fleetingly glimpsed in the experience of personal devotion and love, we can form some idea (and this is our third conclusion) of what the state of eternal fulfillment may mean for us and the world: "God will be all in all" (1 Cor. 15, 28).

These three suggestions combine to produce the following fragmentary picture of heaven even in our earthly life if we analyze human aspiration and love. We take things, events, and persons, in fact our world, with us into our eternal fulfillment. We always remain beings bound up with the world. But if this world is really to be our eternal dwelling, it must be transformed into a loving and open society of man with God. At the same time, however, his creatures will not merge into some undifferentiated unity; their individuality will rather be enhanced and confirmed. Transfigured identity of the world and God in all things are each an indispensable element of heaven. In combination they suggest a condition of final transparency of the world to God, of a world raised forever into affectionate association with God and thus renewed. This also gives some idea of what revelation calls Christ's *pleroma,* the cosmic plenitude of the Body of Christ: Christ built up out of human beings and surrounded by a transfigured world. This provides an initial answer, though still very lacking in detail, to the question of what future fulfillment man's being, and with it the world, is moving towards. We shall try to define this answer more clearly by examining other human aspirations.

Man Created Anew

The second suggestion of what heaven is like emerges from an analysis of man's creative impulse.

Self-Realization of Spirit by Means of the Body

Human development demands not only a selfless attitude but also transforming activity in the world. Self-realization is not what is directly aimed at here, but is always implicitly intended as what gives all human activity its personal meaning. Self-realization can in fact only be attained indirectly, by way of objects, the non-self, because though the self is not an object, all activity is directly concerned with objects. A human being creates around him his own domain in the world; this is part of himself and takes its stamp from him. The more powerful and significant this domain, the more unparalleled and important is the self manifested in it. Within this objective domain man exerts an influence, and makes his own interiority part of the objective state of the world. The hidden driving force of the creative impulse is, therefore, the striving for self-realization. Transformation of the world implies the will to self-development.

This will to transformation is, however, accompanied by a strange powerlessness. Our self-realization perpetually breaks down over the opacity of the world of objects. We cannot achieve full self-development because the way to it—the inevitably indirect route via the objective world—is blocked by a wall. The impenetrability of objective reality can be indicated relatively easily by the example of our bodies, which are what is most immediately objective for us. Involved in corporeality, we are shut off from ourselves. By attaching itself to material things, and exerting its own power in them, our spirit itself is obscured and loses the unencumbered, ready capacities to will, know, and love, which are essential characteristics of spirit. This imposes a restriction on its life: a biologically and psychologically conditioned corporeality, a complex of determinisms and ties which constitute an alien material on which spirit wears itself to death, yet cannot fully raise into the full light of its own personality or ever fully integrate into itself as person.

Spatial limitation also affects the spirit. Involved in corporeality, it no longer exists in the all-embracing, pancosmic relationship which belongs to its spiritual nature; instead, it is confined to a circumscribed spatial domain in which it is one object among others.

Embodied spirit is also subject to temporal limitation. It cannot actuate its full ontological capacity at any single moment of a life plunged in the shadow of corporeality. Consequently, it thrusts forward, wants to have more time, stretches out beyond the present moment into a still unknown future, and as a result never has any real present in which it can simply *be*.

24

Death then shows the full powerlessness of the spirit's attempt to integrate the body into its own immortal nature. Having formed one substance with the body, the spirit is subject to the necessity of having to die. For death does not concern only the bodily "side" of man's total reality, but the substantial unity itself. Death therefore reduces the spirit to total powerlessness. At the same time, however, it must also be affirmed (in a dialectical statement) that the spirit is not dragged down by corporeality into destruction. Nevertheless, in view of this powerlessness of the spirit manifested in death, man's creative impulse is condemned from the start to failure. Yet this does not alter the ontological requirement that the spirit has to transform the body and give a wholly personal character to material reality, for spiritual self-realization is conditional upon this.

A first conclusion follows from this. Since the only way man can achieve self-realization is for spirit to be communicated to what is not spirit, and since spirit nevertheless by its very nature strives for total conscious self-presence as postulated by its very essence as spirit, there must be a state in which spirit can attain total self-realization by means of the body. This in turn implies that the body will cease to be in any way alien to spirit and that spirit will attain its own full realization as spirit.

God's Will in Us

We can only form some further idea of what kind of condition heaven must involve after we have followed out the dialectic of the creative impulse into its complementary assertion. The very struggle to spiritualize matter, which is apparently futile and condemned to failure in death, itself shows how much youthful vigor and unfulfilled expectation there is in man. Perpetual

25

lack of success in his earthly life only intensifies his longing for perfect fulfillment. The fact that no frustration ever holds him back from trying to achieve what defies achievement shows that in aspiration he has already overcome failure.

This will to attempt the unattainable seems to be an essential feature of modern Christian spirituality as we find it expressed, for example, in the works of Reinhold Schneider. He defines the character of Elizabeth of Thuringia, for whom he had a high esteem, precisely by that trait. "For the Christian, she [St. Elizabeth] is a sign of the consuming unattainability of Christianity. What she wanted was impossible of achievement. But she dared to attempt it."

The fact that man is filled to the utmost with aspiration and longing fundamentally means that in hope he is already filled with reality. He is always reaching out for a condition which of himself he cannot attain but in which alone he finds his authentic self. Anyone who realizes and suffers from the fragmentary, conflicting, and helpless character of his life already bears the promise of serene fulfillment in the core of his fragile existence. Man is impelled in everything by a great lack of modesty which has become second nature to him. His very essence is to reach out. He has a downright hunger for a finer future, a more perfect reality.

The constant difference between desire and achievement produces a hopeless terrestrial condition which with Pascal (cf. the great Fragment 72 of *Pensées*) might be described as follows: "We burn with desire to find a firm basis and a final enduring foundation on which to build a tower rising to infinity, but our whole foundation collapses and earth opens to its depths." Pascal calls this condition man's "disproportion," that is, his incongruity. For man lives a profound contradiction, because, though a finite

26

being, he is aware of infinity within him. This might be called the "virtual infinity of the finite." The human mind faces an open horizon of reality yet can never reach and grasp this infinity by his own activity. Human action always springs from a polarity between actual limits and virtual infinity.

This is of fundamental significance. All activity and self-realization is essentially a search for the presence of an infinite. In the ultimate analysis it is an endeavor to be with God. The finite activity by which we endeavor to be really ourselves proves to be a search for God. Man's true will is therefore to will what is divine. But we can only will what is divine if we bear God's will in us. Our aspiration for the infinite is itself God's will in us.

A second conclusion follows from this. Man's creative impulse when perfectly fulfilled renounces its own creation and abandons itself totally to God's activity. Man attains self-realization by being brought to perfect fulfillment by God.

Radical Participation in God's Omnipotence

Man's deepest will therefore involves a double postulate. On the one hand, man must realize himself completely (with soul and body). On the other hand, since he cannot achieve this himself, he must accomplish his full self-realization on God's basis, by allowing himself to be produced by God even in the slightest impulse of his existence. Is this a contradiction? Can our action be an entirely human activity yet equally entirely God's work? Only if these two requirements are combined and harmonized is the specifically human possible. Man can really be himself only if he collaborates in creating himself by a creative power given him by God. Only by a radical participation in God's omnipotence of this kind can man develop the highest ontological activity which accords with what he is. Only a grace-given, super-natural participation in God's creative activity gives man the power to bring his nature to perfect fulfillment.

A body produced by man's divinized creative power would no longer set any limits to the life of the human spirit. The corporeal would then simply be the spiritual taking full effect. A body so formed would be subject to no spatial limitations. Corporeality would involve that profound and constant communication with the universe as a whole which belongs to the very nature of spirit.

A body of that kind would impose no temporal limitations on the spirit. At every moment it would be able to assume and express the plenitude of the spirit. Corporeality of this kind, produced by man himself sharing in God's creative power, transparent to the spirit, pancosmic, and present, is the goal and content of men's creative impulse and represents man's full self-realization.

Full self-realization is therefore a sharing in God's creative activity. But since man's corporeal nature is essentially part and parcel of the world, the world itself must likewise be produced by man's creative collaboration. The world too must become the object of man's action given creative efficacy by participation in God's creative activity.

A third conclusion follows. Man can achieve total fulfillment, but only by sharing in God's creative power. The objects of this human creativity, given as a grace by God, are the human body and the world as a whole. Heaven, therefore, means participation in God's creative activity.

If we combine the three conclusions arrived at in this section of our meditation, the following idea of heaven emerges. A new world will come about through human activity raised beyond and above itself by participation in God's creative power. This will be the eternal home of the transformed body and of the spirit which will have attained its full reality in it. Only a short step will lead our thought to the mystery that, since God's being is identical with his activity, man will share in God's being, with body and soul, and so will the world produced by man in virtue of God's power. Here we reach the boundary of philosophic reflection on heaven. We have caught a glimpse of the mystery of mysteries as goal and content of the human creative impulse— the divinization of the universe.

Perpetual Advance into God

A third philosophical pointer to heaven is to be found in the inner dialectic of human freedom.

Heaven as Eternal Transformation

Human existence might be defined as provisional, preparatory, and cumulative. Man does not develop of necessity to his full capacity. He has as it were to compose his own reality by his own actions. Hence the word "cumulative." It is only by personal action that he begins to be human in the full sense. He has to struggle to become himself. He only finds his way to the innermost core of his own humanity by freely assuming responsibility for himself and freely determining his own destiny.

Man is therefore essentially a nature in process of becoming (*substantia potentialis,* as the Scholastics say). Finite freedom intrinsically implies incompleteness, and therefore man's free nature is involved in an open process of development. Man can never be finished. By the very fact of recognizing that he is free, we have defined him as not yet developed, not yet complete. At the same time, we imply that he can never attain perfect identity with himself, never bridge the gap within him. He can never enter into full possession of his own promise. He is incapable of grasping the full range of his own reality. His activity always leaves an undetermined residue beyond the reach of his own free self-creation. What he is is not yet disclosed, for he is still free, that is, subject to self-determination. Consequently, he is conscious of himself as essentially incomplete, existentially provisional.

But this provisional character of our being is not itself contingent. It is inalienably rooted in the very freedom of a finite being. All freedom, even finite, is absolute. In its ontological ground (though not in its effects) to the extent that it is freedom, it involves absence of necessity. Precisely as such, this does not admit of greater or less. The absolute character of the freedom of a finite being has always fascinated the thought of the West. In this insight of his philosophy of freedom ("Freedom in essence does not admit of more or less"), Thomas Aquinas was closer to a Bernard of Clairvaux, Descartes, and Sartre—the philosophers of radical freedom—than people are generally inclined to admit.

This absolute character of finite freedom means, however, that man, as an intrinsically provisional reality, reaches down to unfathomable depths by the very root of his development; there is not and cannot be anything deeper. Even God's freedom, regarded from this formal point of view, is no "deeper." This shows that human capacity for development (the existentially provisional character of our being) is an absolute element in our creaturely reality itself. To the extent that he is free, therefore, and because he is free, man can never come to the end of his own development. What is absolute in him is beyond the grasp even of the Absolute. Man's eternity must therefore be understood as an open process of becoming, as eternally provisional and cumulative. The absolute character of man's freedom raises him absolutely above any state of completion. He cannot ever be constituted completely and totally. This characteristic can be a bitter torment in his earthly life. At the same time, however, it is the condition of the very possibility of his eternal happiness.

A first conclusion concerning the state of perfect fulfillment would therefore be that heaven cannot be thought of as a static condition. Man's perfect realization must fulfill his very provisionality. The happiness of heaven, therefore, consists in a continual process of transformation.

Freedom Requires the Irrevocable

The absolute freedom of a finite being means that even when it has attained perfect fulfillment it is still advancing and is never definitively fixed. On the other hand, freedom must nevertheless be the ontological ground of finality. For freedom means more than being able to do anything whatsoever at any moment. Our freedom always aims at positing something final, unrepeatable, eternal; in other words, it seeks to rise beyond its open process of development onto the plane of perfect achievement. By turning to some being in an act of existential affirmation, freedom (the proper name of which in its deepest sense is, after all, love) raises this being out of the realm of the conditioned and provisional and places it in an unconditional and irrevocable perspective. It affirms this beloved person to be the partner of its very life: For me you are unique, eternal, and final; the whole framework of the world has meaning for me only through you, with

31

you, and in you (the great prayer of praise and the Amen of the Canon of the Mass: *per ipsum et cum ipso et in ipso* is surely the very language of intensest love). A world without you would be futile and empty for me. Therefore I cannot and will not ever have a different attitude towards you. I shall always be as I am now, loving you, positively willing you to be.

In this free affirmation something definitive occurs, impossible to go back on. The profoundest aim of freedom is to will the beloved with an unconditional, final, and eternal will. It would like to ensure the eternal continuance of what it wills. And freedom even fixes itself in unconditional fulfillment—in relation to the beloved partner it wills to change no more; it wills no longer to be in endless development.

A second conclusion emerges. Human freedom, though always essentially provisional and unfulfilled, aims at finality, fulfillment, eternity, and irrevocability. In other words, it apparently seeks to contradict its own nature.

Ceaseless Renewal in Perfect Fulfillment

This tension implicit in freedom manifests something of the structure of the eternal fulfillment of freedom. On the one hand, creaturely freedom seeks unlimited development, yet at the same time complete finality. In other words, freedom demands to be eternally unfulfilled while at the same time longing for eternal fulfillment. The only logically possible realization of these two divergent demands of freedom woud be a condition in which freedom was totally fulfilled with God's being. All the capacities and possibilities of freedom would at once be totally realized by God, raised to a condition of perfect achievement. At the same time, however, the very fulfillment itself would so increase the creature's capacity to receive, that freedom itself a moment later would be capable of being fulfilled even more by God's being.

The inner dialectic of freedom suggests that our state of eternal fulfillment, heaven, is to be thought of as an uninterrupted advance into God, a perpetual growth into the realms of reality which belong to God alone. Total willing consent to God giving himself would impel freedom to even greater and even more total affirmation of God. That, in fact, is an inherent characteristic of love even on earth; any fulfillment is only the beginning of even greater fulfillment. This dialectic of eternal happiness could only come to an end if freedom were wholly to coincide with divinity. But this can never happen, because of the immeasurability and infinity of the divine nature, and so it continues for ever. The intrinsic dynamism of created freedom points to unceasing renewal in perfect fulfillment as characteristic of heaven.

Heaven as Immediate Contact with God

If we are to describe more closely this continual advance into God, we must reflect on another vital impulse which reveals the depths of our nature, longing for light.

God as Correlate of Knowledge

All spheres of human life are dominated by a longing for "light." This basic impulse is chiefly fulfilled by cognition, which might be described as the inner illumination of the knower. Our being is not yet "pellucid" but is "enlightened" in each of its acts of cognition, as it receives light. Human cognition can only occur by a correlation of knower and known. What is known, by its very nature, is a vis-à-vis, an *ob-jectum*. It is clear, therefore, that our own reality is illuminated only in the light of an object known. Yet the object is itself illuminated only in the cognitive relationship. The mind throws light on the object by knowing it. By throwing light on the object, our mind itself receives light and is itself enlightened. It is only what we give away that we really possess. Our longing for light, for inner enlightenment, is therefore actually a desire to recognize in what is not the self its priority, independent being and identity. The inner drive for clarity produces object and detached objectivity. But since cognition is an expression of that deep reality for which we use the evocative word "heart" (a remnant of the basic insights of biblical metaphysics, embodied in the phrase "the heart of man sees God"), we shut off by it the innermost core of our nature, our heart itself, from others, from the non-self. This explains the solitude of cognition and also the loneliness of the life of thought.

First conclusion: Cognition always involves separation, detachment, and delimitation. Even in heaven the actual reality to which our cognition is directed must remain an *ob-jectum*. For cognition, God always remains a vis-à-vis.

God's Presence in the Knowing Mind

This reminder of the objectivity of knowledge touches only one side of human cognition. Knowledge means possessing as one's own what is other than oneself; what is external is accomplished in an interior action. Cognition therefore requires not only an object but also, and just as fundamentally, a union of knower and known. The opposition between subject and object has to be overcome. From this point of view the duality of knower and known is subsequent and derivative, formed on the basis of a prior identity. But how can subject and object form a unity prior to their duality? Certainly not by the knower having prior possession of the object of knowledge in an actual act of cognition. The identity of knower and known can only come about as the union of the knower with that which is common to all intelligible objects and which therefore transcends them singly and collectively: with being.

This identity of the knowing mind with being cannot, however, consist in an actual cognition of the limitless plenitude of being. That would make any further cognitive process of the mind impossible, for the mind's whole capacity for knowing would be completely fulfilled. This identity can only be a non-objective, as yet unactualized, merely virtual knowledge by the mind of indeterminate being, a dynamic anticipation of the plenitude of being, in other words, an orientation towards union with the limitless. This dynamic union (virtually operative but not experienced) of the created mind with the plenitude of reality produces a fundamental identity between knower and known, on the basis of which alone an intentional demarcation between the two, that is, conceptual cognition, becomes possible.

In the ultimate analysis this characteristic of our finite cognition means that the process of illuminating the object (through which our own inner enlightening takes place) is none other than the creative presence of God within the cognitive process. Reality can be grasped by our mind because it rises into the sphere of our existence out of the full light of God, and because we always (though unreflectingly) have our being in God's light. In every act of cognition God's being is immanent in us, non-conceptually. Consequently, everything objective is already "known" to us. The dynamic immanence in our mind of the absolute plenitude of being prior to actual knowledge of an object makes possible that union between knower and known which is the sole basis on which something external can be attained in an interior act. Cognition always means union and identity.

Our second conclusion will therefore be that cognition is interiorization, in fact antecedent union with what is known. This is possible because we already have a non-conceptual knowledge of objects through God's presence in the knowing mind, because they are thus already present in us. God is "given" to the mind in cognition.

The Mind Already Lives in Direct Relation with God

This dialectic of human cognition, of which only the most general and most readily accessible features could be indicated here, makes possible one of the boldest affirmations about the nature of our eternal fulfillment, heaven. We have shown that the two polarities (ob-ject and identity) which are the conditions of objective knowledge, can only come about because God makes himself present to the mind. This presence of God in the mind is only lived non-conceptually; it is not known explicitly as such. We know things in God's light, and thus are ourselves enlightened. The infinite mediates the finite to our minds and the finite mediates us to ourselves. God is, therefore, in more immediate contact with the mind than the world of objects is, and this in turn is more present to the mind than the mind is to itself. The mind is mediated to itself by the world and the world is mediated to the mind by God. The mind therefore lives already (though unconsciously, non-conceptually, and implicitly) in direct relation with God. The dynamism which impels it towards perfect knowledge and consequently towards perfect inner illumination, contains an even more fundamental drive towards the perfect actuation of its direct relation to God. Objects would only be assumed with perfect objectivity into our interior enlightenment if our mind were to actuate its already existing direct relation to God, in conscious explicit direct cognition.

Direct relationship with God known and grasped—that is the goal to which the whole cognitive dialectic of the finite mind tends. Direct relationship with God would mean, however, that the ontological act of the finite mind knowing him would be the reality of God himself. For in every explicit act of objective cognition, a third element is formed between knower and known, an inner bond (what the Scholastics called the *species*). This unites both knower and known, so that the two are truly one and the same. In the case of God's immediate presence known and grasped, this inner bond can only be the infinite reality of God himself. God's immediate presence cannot be mediated to our mind by anything finite.

Our third conclusion and summary will therefore be that a real union of man with God's being is involved in the direct intellectual grasp of God's presence which the dialectic of finite cognition requires for its ultimate fulfillment. But this concerns not merely the intellectual plane but the innermost core of our finite nature. For cognition is, as we have already recalled, an act produced from the inner depth of human reality, of the "heart." At the same time, however, it must not be forgotten that conceptual knowledge always implies an object and, therefore, detachment and demarcation. Although the creature receives God's own reality in the act of having God as the immediate object of knowledge, it remains totally outside God's reality. It remains radically a creature. One further remark in conclusion. The world is always mediated to us by God's light. If the human mind (in

37

heaven) perceives this light directly, it consciously attains its awareness of the world as an element in its union with God's being. Now cognition produces a profound assimilation of knower and known. Knowledge of the world by man in his state of perfect fulfillment unites the world with the human being of the knower, which is no other (through heavenly cognition) than that of God. Consequently, when our cognition is brought to perfect fulfillment, God's reality pervades the reality of the world. The whole cosmos is bathed in God's infinite being and so transfigured. These are philosophically conceivable adumbrations of the supernatural mystery which theology calls the beatific vision of God.

We may now sum up in a few key phrases the results of this philosophic meditation on the fundamental structure of heaven, which is intended to form the basis of all the considerations which follow. From the polarity of human cognition we have surmised a state by which God's being becomes ours. With the help of the dialectic of human freedom we have seen that this union with God's being involves an uninterrupted and eternal advance further into God. In this constantly growing self-abandonment to the superabundant richness of God's life, our domination over ourself and the world increases to such an extent—as the dialectic of the human urge to create appeared to suggest—that we become capable, in virtue of creative power conferred on us by God, of collaborating in producing our corporeality and the world of nature. Finally, we inferred from the dialectic of human self-giving and devotion that the powerfully creative state of perpetually growing immediate relationship to God will make the whole cosmos transparent to God.

These are ontological prefigurations of that perfect fulfillment that totally transcends our powers, but that we nevertheless aspire to with all the longing of our human nature, prefigurations of totally realized communion of life with the risen Christ, that is, of heaven.

We have attempted to trace the main outlines of the complete and total realization of all man's potentialities. This has given us some idea of what it means when it is said that God incarnate came "into his own" (Jn. 1, 11). He is no stranger to our world, to our experiences, to anything that happens to us and befalls us. All of it is pervaded by an inner meaning centered on God made man, in a dynamism that points towards the incomprehensible. We want to try to decipher this meaning, feature by feature, in six meditations. Then, finally, in our last consideration, we shall risk the attempt to give a total interpretation of man's lot: life and death, joy and grief, happiness and sorrow inclusive. If we can succeed in expounding what our hope means, it will become clear, even where we have to draw rigorous distinctions and make stern decisions, that an even greater hope forms the vital center of all we can say.

2

Hope Understood

In the Letter to the Romans, Paul, who on occasion could express himself with astonishing simplicity, reduced the basic demands of hope to a simple formula: "Rejoice in your hope, be patient in tribulation, be constant in prayer" (Rom. 12, 12). These are very inconspicuous features of Christian witness—joy, patience, and constancy. But something unfathomable takes place in them, which Paul describes in the words "aglow with the spirit" (Rom. 12, 11). How does merely living our human life, in joy, patience, and constancy, come to bear radiant witness to God? How does our everyday routine become a sign of the Absolute in the world? How does our simple expectation of a better life become hope and anticipation of an eternal fulfillment?

Hope has to be learned afresh. We have to examine just what it is we aspire to. A good deal of our dreaming amounts to nothing but commonplace and debilitating escapism. But a small fraction is an authentic stimulus which prevents us from coming to terms with things as they are but should not be. It is important, as Ernst Bloch repeatedly emphasizes, to get a better knowledge of this authentic core of hope and to direct our innermost impulse unswervingly to the right goal. In other words, our daily hopes have to be transformed into a conscious conception of hope. On every plane of his life, man seeks what is not yet fully conscious and not yet achieved. In this meditation we shall consider human dreams, the vision of far-away beauty, a world of longing and aspiration revealed in every kind of situation and on every level of human development.

Life as Imagined Hope

The child grows up by dreaming and imagining. Fairy tales, myths, and legends are commonly regarded nowadays as archetypes of human hope. They reveal the realms from which our psyche unconsciously draws its life, and which we enter as soon as our everyday self opens even a little to its own depths. Life is, in fact, fundamentally, quintessential childhood. If we deprive a child of imaginative tales, we not merely rob him of enchantment, but destroy the life of his psyche and his future development. For in the ultimate analysis man is only truly human when he reaches what is beyond his grasp and incomprehensible. Where do I come from? Where am I going? What is the ultimate meaning of my life? Those are the basic questions for authentic human life. Now fairy tales and legends, these first spontaneous foreshadowings of hope give quite precise answers to these ultimate questions. All through life, perhaps, people may not be able to add much more to them. We shall try to unfold a few of these basic fairy-tale answers. This will show why such myths and legends are at bottom a manifestation of hope.

The Origin of Human Life

What happens in a fairy tale, if we reduce it to essentials? Not much, really, except the only thing that matters. Usually these stories begin happily. Then the threat of evil enters in. Next, evil appears to triumph once and for all. But then man receives inexplicable help and strength from some wonderful realm of reality. Finally, the weak human being defeats the power of evil and lives happily ever after.

Everyone feels, hearing stories of this kind, that that is how things are, or rather, that is how they must be. Why? We do not know and cannot give any incontrovertible reasons why it should be so. That does not really matter. The main point is the spiritual view or intuition of reality. From fairy tales the child has already learned its catechism beforehand. It is quite clear to the child that mankind was once perfectly happy, then came the fall and the domination of evil, followed by a supernatural deliverance, and finally the world opened out on lasting happiness. All this involves insight into the ultimate features of reality. This must not be misunderstood. We are not trying to place religion and metaphysics on the same level as fairy tale, myth, and legend. The latter are simply a door that must be opened if we are to reach the realm of mystery where it becomes possible to interpret the meaning of life. Every religion teacher knows how hard children find it to understand the history of salvation if they have never heard fairy tales and stories at home.

It is not surprising, then, that Marxism has not been able to dispense with the same kind of service from fairy tales in seeking to bring home the meaning of its earthly eschatology. In the "little red book," *Quotations from Chairman Mao Tse-tung,* we find the following remarkable story. "There is an ancient Chinese fable called 'The Foolish Old Man Who Removed the Mountains.' It tells of an old man who lived in northern China long, long ago and was known as the Foolish Old Man of North Mountain. His house faced south and beyond his doorway stood the two great peaks, Taihang and Wangwu, obstructing the way. With great determination he led his sons in digging up these mountains hoe in hand. Another greybeard, known as the Wise

Old Man, saw them and said derisively, 'How silly of you to do this! It is quite impossible for you few to dig up these two huge mountains.' The Foolish Old Man replied, 'When I die, my sons will carry on; when they die, there will be my grandsons, and then their sons and grandsons, and so on to infinity. High as they are, the mountains cannot grow any higher and with every bit we dig, they will be that much lower. Why can't we clear them away?' Having refuted the Wise Old Man's wrong view, he went on digging every day, unshaken in his conviction. God was moved by this, and he sent down two angels, who carried the mountains away on their backs." Mao's application follows: "Today, two big mountains lie like a dead weight on the Chinese people. One is imperialism, the other is feudalism . . ." The rest does not concern us here.

After the foregoing we have no hesitation in saying that fairy tales give imaginative expression to what is, in fact, genuine experience of the primordial events of the world and of mankind. That is why such stories are so clear, convincing, and intuitively comprehensible. The child still gazes at mundane reality at a depth where the drama of man's history is directly present —where, when an apple is eaten without permission, the world is plunged into catastrophe; if a word is forgotten, towns are destroyed; if a box is opened, all kinds of evil escape. These events are symbols that being human is not a question of giving and taking, but is determined by relationships which cannot be understood on the plane of equality and equivalence.

The Unique Value of Reality

In one of the finest fairy tales of recent times, *The Little Prince* by Antoine de Saint-Exupéry, we read: "If you were to say to the grown-ups: 'I saw a beautiful house made of rosy brick, with geraniums in the windows and doves on the roof,' they would not be able to get any idea of that house at all. You would have to say to them: 'I saw a house that cost $20,000.' Then they would exclaim: 'Oh, what a pretty house that is!'" Here we see something essential expressed by the fairy tale—things are valuable because they are unique, not because they can be measured and compared. In a fairy tale, the world appears as it really ought to be, in fact as it already is in its innermost core—a world where one can talk about forests, stars, butterflies, and roses, and does not necessarily (as Saint-Exupéry rather quaintly puts it) have to talk "sensibly" about bridge, golf, politics, and neckties.

Another point. The fairy tale is an inner world where truth is goodness, goodness is beauty, and beauty is power. It might even be defined as a story in which good always prevails. Now that is true; it is genuine metaphysics. That is to say, in the real realm, in the background, that is really so, despite all appearance to the contrary in the foreground. A fairy story contains the whole teaching of the *philosophia perennis* about the transcendentals: Being is true, good, one, and beautiful. One can only point this out; it is never possible to give a demonstrative proof. These relationships which are concealed by the foreground can only be "seen" with the heart.

In everyday experience that is not how things are. There may be a glimmer of beauty even in what is evil, confused, indifferent, or stupid. But that is only seemingly so, the fairy tale assures us. And it is so only because our heart is not as it should be. Beauty is really the way in which reality assumes an expressive character for the heart. If our heart is in confusion, even confused things can influence us. Legend shows us a way out of this superficial disorder, for it presents a realm of metaphysical experiences where light shines in the darkness, and where reality, not appearance, summons us.

The Power of Spirit

Another very significant insight embodied in these tales is that witches are ugly and wrinkled not because they are old but because they are wicked. They do not come under the power that could make them eternally beautiful. They live outside the sphere of what is really creative and constructive. They can, of course, bewitch and produce surprising novelties. But their creations are mere semblance, whatever their momentary power.

What is real and lasting always springs from the power of good. In fairytales that power is always boundless. The steep rock in the wilderness is a marvelous castle; it only needs to be touched by a breath of the spirit and it becomes what it has secretly been all along. There is no limit to metamorphosis—at the twelfth stroke of midnight the coach becomes a pumpkin. The idea or the process of creation does not need to be "represented" in these stories for the "creative principle" to be intuitively grasped. It is sufficient to realize that a power is at work in the world which is capable of bringing the greater out of the less, knows no limits, and is able to transform things at will. And that is so because ultimately everything good is related, everything has the same origin, everything is united in God. In everything dormant forms are ready to spring to life and blossom heavenwards. These are all insights unsurpassable by any philosophy or interpretation of life. They are universally valid truths about reality.

The Future

Time and time again we read in fairytales: "They lived happily ever after and had a large family." That is the way nearly all fairy tales end, and it is the end of the story or, rather, of history itself. The end is as absolute as the beginning ("Once upon a time there was . . ."). Fruitfulness is the end. That is apparently all there is to be said. Marriage is the end of the story. A perfect, ideal, and symbolic marriage, the archetype of the nuptials of the Creator with his creation.

But something else had happened first. Cinderella had left the kitchen, the princess had been wakened from sleep with a kiss, the seven ravens had laid aside their black plumage, a crystal palace had come down from on high, the witches had been thrown into the abyss. In other words, a judgment had taken place in which the secrets of hearts were laid bare. A world of eternal creativity came into existence, a realm in which our dreams and aspirations, our constant anticipation of a world set right, began to be realized. All that already amounts to a vision of the apocalypse or, rather perhaps, implies a spontaneous intuition of it. Even the real meaning of the idea of recompense is there. There is no merely external, adventitious reward superimposed on man, or added like a veneer. Eternal life is the full development of man's innermost reality, the domain of his own heart. That is why fairy tales and legends contain in germ a whole eschatological ethic, the only ethic which is valid in Christian thought.

A World Set Right

At bottom, legend is concerned with hope, the most radical thing in human life. Why do people tell the story of a threat that had to be overcome? Why do the characters in such tales achieve happiness only by undergoing many trials? Why is love described conquering death, or a bewitched person brought back to genuine life? Unmistakably these are happenings that can be interpreted

46

and evaluated only in terms of salvation. Sometimes it is one of seven brothers or a simple farmer's son, more often a young prince disguised as a farmer's son or shepherd, whose kiss wakens the sleeping princess forever (or brings her back to life?). The "saviour" has to undergo sufferings and perform feats. He is attacked by evil powers, has to wander all over the world, descend into the abyss. A host of strange and remarkable beings assist him, good fairies and dwarfs, old women and wise old men.

This is no chance matter. Since the very dawn of creation the image of Christ has been stamped on the human soul's very being, for that creation was made in him, through him, and by him (cf. Col. 1, 15–23). It is all a translation of a profound longing for a purity, deliverance, and salvation, which have to be bestowed on man because somewhere or other he has lost them.

Being as Companionship

In fairy tale and legend love is strong. In fact it is the only thing that is strong. In Hans Andersen's *The Snow Queen,* little Kay is pierced through and through by inhuman cold, the coldness of pure intelligence. But little Gerda finds him. The warmth of her tears melts her friend's heart, which has been turned to ice; the forgotten word is found once more and all is saved. Love has power over the evil that threatens another person. Fear cannot lay hold of them; they wander hand in hand through terrifying, danger-haunted forests. It is always a couple, a simple, innocent, and happy pair, who are able to save one another. One without the other would not be half as strong, would, in fact, be nothing.

Now all these things are statements about the fundamental

constitution of human reality. Man only becomes human by sharing his life, by sociability and communication. Living a human life involves truly personal relations. And that means that in mutual love one partner receives himself as gift from the other and himself bestows a similar reality in return. So much so that his very life depends on the beloved, and love can call back the dead to life. And so it is that fairytales awaken in the child the primordial conviction of love which is latent in every human being. Perhaps no one has ever encountered the power of love as fairy tale presents it. That kind of love can perhaps never be met with in life at all, for its scope is infinitely greater than human relationships, which are liable to disappointments; behind it lies something infinite. These are insights that philosophers have been struggling for for centuries without really getting much farther than children's fairytales.

We have spoken of six fairy-tale themes that interpret human life, and have drawn attention to features by which they open a door into spiritual reality. Many more could be found. For example, the symbolism of objects and events, the special way in which they interpret knowledge, power, age, death, and childhood (the fundamental human realities). They are all presentiments in which the soul of a child opens out to the absolute and is brought into the presence of the fundamental reality. Without legend and fairy tale we should perhaps have lost the sense of mystery.

Personal Life as Explicitly Conscious Hope

Fairytales, as we have just seen, serve to mediate the future; they have an eschatological function. Ernst Bloch, in his book

The Principle of Hope, attempts to raise the dynamism of hope, which is inherent in man, to the plane of conscious exercise. He shows that even in the unregulated and uncomprehending desires of the ordinary man, an anticipatory consciousness is at work; light is breaking ahead. The child grasps at everything in an endeavor to find what it really means. At one time a boy wants to be an engineer, at another a baker's boy. He wants to live a finer life than perhaps his father does. Something simply has to be found which others have not yet been able to find. But even later, desires do not decrease, though what is wished for narrows down. The dynamism of aspiration, grown older, aims nearer, is more explicit and settled. But, as ever, something important and essential is lacking, and imagination is not dead. By day and night it conjures up the desirable, what might have been, what should have been. Man allows himself remarkably easily, at any phase of life, to be taken unawares by the unexpected. It is as though no situation in life is so good that it could not be abandoned at any moment. The search for something better goes on, however long the obstacles persist. Aspirations all aim at what is not yet known, the unachieved, unfulfilled, utopian. In them man's nature reacts, ripostes—what is crooked must be made straight, the half must become the whole.

But what, Ernst Bloch asks, is the structure of a consciousness that can dream in this way? Two basic characteristics may be noted, the opacity of momentary experience and the gleam of light ahead. The pulse of life beats in us, inaudible but present, surmised. What is most obscure is the present moment of experience. Direct experience is least accessible. There is no light at the foot of the lighthouse. At the point of immediate contact everything is still opaque. What is impending and longed for, however, is far enough away for the ray of consciousness to be

49

able to throw light on it. This reveals the strange fact that no one is actually fully present, no one is really living. At the same time, something is driving us out into the open, away from the opaque proximity of things. Directly here and now as we are, we are empty and therefore avid, straining and restless. None of us chose this impelling condition. It has been with us since birth, by the very fact that we exist. What is not yet expresses itself in what we are, as a "hunger," as aim, intention, longing, desire, daydreams, and all the imagining of what we still have not got.

All longing implies a refusal of what is actually there. Consequently, our desire becomes an explosive force against the prison of deprivation. Hope refuses to sleep. Even in the despairing, hope is not totally absent. Even the suicide flees to negation as a refuge of peace and rest. The fact that it is possible to indulge in dreams shows the importance of what is still open and unde termined in man himself. Man invents imaginary wishes for himself and finds vast materials within himself for the purpose. The brute animals have nothing comparable. Man alone is less dense and compact. Something has remained unfulfilled in him, an empty space has opened out in reality. Dreams and longings fill it, and much that cannot turn outwards turns restlessly within. The one thing necessary but still to come is mirrored under many forms in our world of what has already come to be. The pleasure in disguise, adventure stories, absorption in reading, dancing, acting, and daydreaming generally—all this is full of imaginary shapes and forms of longing. Is it all mere illusion? Perhaps it would be more comfortable to forget longing, but where would that take us? The desire to have things better, more beautiful, or simply different, never dies. Longing is indestructible, rooted in the human craving for happiness. Man's very nature is expressed in the optative—"If only things were different!"

What is the ultimate content and direction of all these longings? Undoubtedly the ultimate goal of what men strive for everywhere is their native place, so to speak. That is what is still unfound, the sum of aspiration, the as yet unknown, what lies obscurely at the root of all daydreams and endeavors. All expressions of hope converge on one indefinable center, some symbols of which are, for example, self-possession, intensity of being, ultimate union of man with his aspiration, ultimate self-identity without alienation, ultimate peace with maximum intensity of awareness and participation.

This goal of hope is still masked in us, the general goal of the will is still not ascertained. The absolute is present to us only as expectation, as predisposition for something, tendency towards something. Those who hope are still living in what might be called the prehistory of their true reality. Man only understands what he is from his dynamic orientation towards a still open goal. His essence is not what has been. On the contrary, man's essence is still being fought for; it has to be conquered. Man's humanity still lies ahead. His authentic reality is not yet achieved, he only possesses it in hope. Man's real genesis is not at the beginning, but begins afresh again and again in those who hope. The absolute pitch of ultimate fulfillment is most magnificently indicated in Paul's words: "What no eye has seen, nor ear heard, nor the heart of man conceived, what God has prepared for those who love him" (1 Cor. 2, 9). That is the promise of uttermost hope. Heaven is the quintessential meaning of human development.

One of the noblest and as yet unfulfilled tasks of theology is to work out the functions of human hope in shaping life, determining history, and even in creating reality. It must throw light on the intrinsic dynamism of human reality. Fundamentally, man is constantly dreaming of heaven. It is precisely because he does so that he is a human being. Heaven is, therefore, always present in the depths of human consciousness, as what makes human growth in awareness and the forward movement of history possible at all, as what is constantly and everywhere foreshadowed but still unreached. The forces operative in the world are flowing in man towards something radically new. Has Christianity ever before understood its own truth so clearly?

Christianity as a Religion of Hope

One becomes a Christian by the sacrament of baptism. Now, baptism is also essentially the sacrament of hope. Nowadays astonishingly little is said about this. It was different in the early Church. In those days the great teachers of the faith delivered long homilies, so-called "initiations into the mystery" (mystagogic catecheses). They explained the mystery of Christian life by means of Old Testament events, readings in which God's great deeds (*magnalia Dei*) in the Old Testament were recalled to the candidates for baptism. We still hear a few of these readings even today in the liturgy of the Paschal Vigil, which is actually the Church's baptismal liturgy. The mystery of baptism and that of the resurrection are closely linked in the Christian faith. The mysteries of the Old Testament contain fundamental human experience. If we are to grasp the mystery of hope and to transform it into an explicitly conscious hope, we must necessarily have recourse to them. In the mystagogic catechetics of the Fathers of the Church, five symbols of baptism constantly recur.

Creation as Exemplar of the New Creation in Baptism

The Fathers regarded the creation of the world as the model or exemplar of that re-creation of the cosmos which Christ brought us by his resurrection and which we enter by the sacrament of baptism. In Genesis we read: "In the beginning God created the heavens and the earth. The earth was without form and void, and darkness was upon the face of the deep; and the spirit of God was moving over the face of the waters. And God said, 'Let there be light'" (Gen. 1, 1–3). The symbolism of this passage was self-evident to the Fathers. Just as at the creation of the world the earth rose out of the waters by the operation of the Spirit of God, so there is a "new creation" with the human being who comes up out of the waters of baptism. Immersion in the water expresses a mysterious process of renewal, an event which is so overwhelming that if it were not for Christ's emphatic words, one would not dare to affirm that in baptism an immersion, a plunge into the divine life, takes place. Through the grace of baptism, God himself dwells in us. With body and soul, with our whole human reality, we have truly put on the risen Christ, the Son of the Father, whose light, the Holy Spirit, hovers above us. A new creation has emerged, the new heaven and the new earth. We have grown together with Christ into a single reality. "Therefore, . . . if any one is in Christ, he is a new creation; the old has passed away, behold, the new has come" (2 Cor. 5, 17). Leonidas, Origen's father, showed his understanding of these depths of the sacrament when he knelt

53

down before his newly baptized son and adored Christ now living in the child.

Deliverance of the World after the Flood

The next symbol in which the Fathers used to contemplate the sacrament of hope was the Flood. The symbolic content of the narrative is the deliverance of the world from total destruction. A single just man is sufficient for God to have mercy on the world. The saints protect the world. There is a mysterious defense, a radiant realm of grace, inhabited even by those who know nothing about it. Noah's righteousness saved the world.

That does not exhaust the symbolic meaning of the story. The Bible describes how God made a new, cosmic covenant with Noah, " 'Behold, I establish my covenant with you and your descendants after you, and with every living creature that is with you, the birds, the cattle, and every beast of the earth with you, as many as came out of the ark. I establish my covenant with you, that never again shall all flesh be cut off by the waters of a flood, and never again shall there be a flood to destroy the earth.' And God said, 'This is the sign of the covenant which I make between me and you and every living creature that is with you, for all future generations: I set my bow in the cloud, and it shall be a sign of the covenant between me and the earth' " (Gen. 9, 9–13). Here we have a covenant made by God, not with a particular nation, but with all humanity and with the whole earth. The cosmos (with the earth as its center, according to the world picture of those times) has entered into the economy of salvation. This covenant is the beginning of a new creation, of a world saved from destruction. By it, nature became part of history, and was drawn into the relationship of love and friendship between God and men. We can understand from this what baptism means for the whole world. What was foreshadowed in Noah was accomplished in Christ. His resurrection had universal efficacy, and by it the world was promised eternal stability and indestructible glory. In the risen Christ the rainbow of eternal hope spanned the whole earth. This promise of a new world, a world healed and wholly native to man, is made to every Christian at baptism, and imposed on him as a task. By his baptism the Christian assumes an obligation to God and the world, that of hoping and of maintaining hope in the world, just as God binds himself that even the world as a whole will never be destroyed but will endure forever. Baptism is God's cosmic sign, not for the individual Christian only but for the whole of humanity and the whole universe. It is tremendous to think that in baptism God approaches the world to make a new heaven and earth; the whole world is groaning in labor, giving birth to heaven (cf. Rom. 8, 18–24).

Exodus from Captivity

The third patristic baptismal symbol is Israel's escape from Egypt, the exodus. The first Easter hymn was sung by the shore of the Red Sea. An oppressed nation fled from captivity, led by the pillar of cloud. The ruler and his chariots set off in pursuit. The people arrived at the sea, and were now exposed to annihilation or renewed enslavement. We must realize the hopelessness of the situation, the distress of the people thronging the shores of the sea. Then we can appreciate the full significance of what happened. For precisely when it was impossible for men to save themselves by their own efforts, God effected what they themselves could not. Moses stretched his hand over the sea and

God commanded the wind; the sea was driven back by a strong east wind. Israel could walk through the sea, the waters standing like walls to right and left. Moses stretched out his hand again and the waters flowed back and engulfed the whole pursuing army. When dawn followed that terrible yet wonderful night, the people realized that they were really free at last, and started to sing the exodus song, "I will sing to the Lord, for he has triumphed gloriously . . ." (Ex. 15, 1–18). We are then told that Aaron's sister Miriam took a timbrel in her hand, and all the women followed her with timbrels and dancing. This great work of God in setting his people free from despair was to remain throughout the centuries the greatest memory in the history of Israel.

We still sing the same hymn even now at the Easter vigil. It is our baptismal hymn. We celebrate symbolically our own deliverance by Christ's resurrection. Christ passes through the realm of death, the sea of affliction, and in the dawn of Easter day emerges from the abyss of human distress. Just as the sea once parted in front of the people of Israel, and the gates of death opened for Christ, so the Christian goes down into the water, crosses the sea of death, leaves what is transitory behind and emerges on the farther shore, the shore of the resurrection. That is how Paul describes what happens in baptism: ". . . all of us who have been baptized into Christ Jesus were baptized into his death, . . . have been united with him in a death like his and . . . shall certainly be united with him in a resurrection like his" (Rom. 6, 3–5). Consequently, the boldest dreams of mankind have been realized in the Christian life. We have become immortal and have broken down the wall of fear. The death that we have still to suffer will simply be the final accomplishment of our baptism, of our Christian hope, final immersion in eternal glory of body and soul.

Entry into the Messianic Promised Land

The crossing of the Jordan by the Jewish people introduces a new symbolic element into our previous understanding of baptism. The people wandered for forty years in the desert of Sinai. Moses died. Joshua took over the leadership. Then came the occupation of the land which in the dreams of Israel was to become the kingdom of God, a realm of messianic promise. The miracle of the dividing of the waters was repeated. The waters coming down from above rose up in a wall, while those flowing down to the Salt Sea completely dried up, and the people passed over dryshod opposite Jericho (Josh. 3, 14–17).

This time it was not a miraculous deliverance from despair but the beginning of a long-drawn-out process, the start of a new conquest, in which the history of the passage of the Jordan becomes a symbol of baptism. In baptism Christ's life is bestowed on us, not in its full development, but as an active potentiality, a tendency, an inner impulsion to transform ourselves on the pattern of Christ. Impelled by this dynamism of grace (which may be bestowed as baptism of water, baptism of blood, or baptism of desire), the Christian is to grow more and more into a community of life with Christ. Paul describes this process in the Letter to the Ephesians: "until we all attain to . . . mature manhood, to the measure of the stature of the fullness of Christ . . . grow up in every way . . . into Christ" (Eph. 4, 13–15).

Baptismal grace is, therefore, not merely a gift but a challenge, something dynamic and impelling. We have, as the apostle teaches, to allow ourselves to be led by it (Rom. 8, 14). Christ wills to be formed in us more and more (cf. Gal. 4, 19). According to this Pauline view, baptismal grace is simply Christian life as a whole, inasmuch as it involves growth into the realm of reality which is that of the risen Christ. In the course of this,

the Christian becomes more and more clearly aware of his communion with Christ, and lives more and more deeply and responsibly the mystery of his resurrection. By his actions, in
conjunction with all the baptized, he builds up the eschatological fullness of Christ, accomplishes a constant renewal until in
death, the last act of his baptism, he finds his ultimate home
in that reality of the risen Christ which comprises the whole universe within it.

Carried Away by the Fiery Whirlwind of the Spirit

In conclusion we must also refer to the image which many
Fathers of the Church regarded as the deepest symbol of the
baptismal mystery—the assumption of the prophet Elijah. The
end came for him after an ardent, consuming prophetic life. He
handed on the prophetic office to his disciple Elisha, then the
two went out into the desert. Elijah worked a miracle, parting
the waters of the Jordan so that they both crossed dryshod.
While they were advancing farther into the desert, a fiery chariot
came and separated them. Elijah was carried off in a whirlwind.
Only his prophet's mantle was left on the sand (2 Kings 2, 1–13).

For man to be carried away by the whirlwind of the Holy
Spirit is indeed the deepest meaning of the sacrament of baptism.
By baptismal grace the Christian already lives in heaven, in a new-
made world of direct relationship to God. This living in heaven
is, of course, not perceptible to the senses. It will only be manifest
at death. Until then the Christian has to become more and
more silent, patient, humble, and kind. This attitude of Christian
maturity brings our baptism to its full growth and represents
hope for the world. The Christian evokes heaven from the hidden depths of the world. Every Christian action—faith, hope,

sacrifice, endurance, bold initiative—brings nearer the heaven which is to come. Consequently, the Christian is the mediator of a universal hope.

Another thought must be put forward at this point. Who is really a Christian? Christians are those who are baptized into, or, rather, penetrated with, the mind and outlook of Christ. They may be human beings who have received the sacrament of baptism in its full form (baptism of water), by the total sacrifice of their lives (baptism of blood), or in the hidden form of a desire not yet explicitly formulated, and perhaps impossible to articulate at all (baptism of desire, or aspiration). Every positive action in life, the most imperceptible impulse towards a brother man, is already an appropriation of the mind of Christ. All such human beings are already members of the Church whether they explicitly realize this or not. In this sense the theological maxim *Extra ecclesiam nulla salus* ("No salvation outside the Church") is one of the most liberating doctrines in the Christian gospel. For if this proposition is converted according to the elementary rules of logic, it assumes a profoundly encouraging form: "Wherever there is salvation, there is the Church." To put it in its simplest form, *Ubi ecclesia, ibi salus—Ubi salus, ibi ecclesia* ("Where Church, there is salvation"—"Where salvation, there is Church"). What makes the visible and tangible Church a special sign among those people who are already living their Christian reality but have not yet expressly recognized themselves to be Christians is above all the witness it bears to hope. The Church is concretely lived eschatological hope, an exodus community, the pilgrim people of God (cf. Heb. 13, 13–14).

It is, therefore, astonishing to see and experience how little in fact Christians consciously live on the thought of heaven, how faint their expectation is. To bear witness to hope is one of the

Christian's essential functions in the world. To perform it requires conscious conviction of the reality of heaven and practice, so to speak, in realizing the presence of heaven. Following Thomas Aquinas, whole generations of Christians were taught that man's ultimate salvation consists in the direct and beatifying vision of God. Probably no one today would dispute that this view was largely drawn from non-biblical and in particular Greek ideas. The New Testament speaks very little of seeing God. It prefers other images to bring home vividly to our minds the final state to be hoped for. It describes the goal of all aspirations as a banquet, marriage, a new cosmos, a new name, a share in the friendship of God. This imagery does not present God as an "object" seen and penetrated in its innermost essence, scrutinized and known, but as a personal being, with whom one enters into loving relationship as one does with persons, and so gradually comes to share in his love by an ever-increasing process of interiorization.

Courage and high-mindedness are needed to think of man in this way, with the ability to make room in one's own heart for the great surge of hope. We live, in fact, in a very small corner of the world. Often enough we are the prisoners of our own pettiness. We are gazing the whole time at the same narrow valleys of our own hopelessness. Even the best of us constantly needs encouragement, human contacts which restore élan and hope. Where are such people to be found, and what part do they play in our life? What do they look like? If we knew that, we could seek fresh strength and renewed youth from them in hours of discouragement. That is what we shall consider in our next meditation.

3

Hope Encountered

At the beginning of the First Letter to Timothy, Paul describes himself as an apostle of hope: "Paul, an apostle of Christ Jesus by command of God our Saviour and of Christ Jesus, our hope" (1 Tim. 1, 1). God's envoy is always a sign of hope for us. In this meditation let us ask ourselves where we actually meet with hope, in what sectors of life, in what human relationships. What are those fundamental human situations which maintain and nourish our aspiration towards an absolute fulfillment? We want to indicate some of the points at which the divine becomes perceptible in human life, and reflect on them from the philosophical and theological points of view. In this way we shall attempt to sketch the fundamental structure of hope as sign. Who is an envoy of hope in our life?

The Child

Hope is characteristic of childhood, which essentially involves emergence into what has not yet come to be. To have an essentially right relation to children therefore means living in close contact with the blessing of hope. We do not mean anything idyllic; we are not forgetting that destructive and terrible things can happen in a child. A child can be a prey to fear and panic; its life may be poisoned by grief. The child can withdraw into loneliness, anger, and embitterment, and fall victim to the enmity of evil desires, revengeful anger, and ingrained hatred. Romano Guardini has warned us not to sentimentalize over the heart of a child; it is far too great and its roots penetrate far deeper into the metaphysical pattern of the world for it to be belittled and trivialized. But terrible things can happen in the life of a child only because it is open to the splendid promise of hope, because it is on the way to God and is therefore exposed to danger.

The child spontaneously lives in a domain where there is always going to be "more." But what is genuinely "more" in human life is divine. From the start the child is increasingly an adumbration of what is to be, an inner dynamism, foretaste, and promise. Precisely because a child is really more than it actually is yet, it reaches out to what is divine, and so can perceive significance and meaning in the world. Its eyes still see everything in an absolute light, in the light of the Absolute, in fact. A tree, a garden, a house, a pond, a candle, a piece of bread, and many other things have profound meaning for a child, and reach far down into the exemplary and symbolic depths of the world. The child still lives in a world of limitless extent because everywhere, in everything, vistas of meaning open out for him. This mysterious world—no longer perceived by us, only caught sight of once again in rare momentary recollections of childhood—wells up from within the child. The gates of reality are not yet closed to him by the practical interest of the moment, or barred by the mind's turning in on itself in reflection. His mind's direct link with the world creates an ontological landscape of its own which is radiant with the glory of God.

Aquinas viewed these features of childhood in the following

way. The first act of intellectual discernment, when reason begins to function, is to apprehend being as a whole. This intellectual intuition puts the child in touch with God and sets all in relation to him. The child lives so fundamentally and spontaneously in God's presence that the very first movement of its rational consciousness is capable of apprehending God (implicitly, of course, and without naming him) as the ultimate ground of all reality (cf. *Summa theologica,* 1a, 2ae, q. 89, art. 6, and parallel passages).

In this connection it may be asked whether this kind of intellectual intuition of God which follows necessarily from the very nature of childhood does not in fact always involve what we earlier referred to as "baptism of desire." If this were so—and we agree with those who affirm that it is—the child would escape, even in the early stage of its growing consciousness, from that obscure condition of remoteness from God which we call "original sin." That would mean that there is no living person who, in principle, is far from the Church; in every human as such, therefore, it is possible to meet a Christian. That would make it clear that God gave himself in sacrifice for all men and has saved them from ruin, even those who outwardly are not of the Church and never want to be, that is to say, all our present world. If we meet such people on this basis, we approach them in a quite different frame of mind—no longer hostile or domineering, or in an attempt at coercion. We should be able to say, tacitly of course: "You too, though you do not want to be one of us at all, are God's beloved creature. What happens in you, human being, non-Christian or atheist, in your heart of hearts, in your conscience and conviction, hope and love, under the influence of the Spirit of God—whom you do not know by name and cannot know—corresponds to our faith. Our faith coincides with what you as an honest human being in your heart of hearts have found to be holy." What changes there will have to be before we can speak like this in all honesty! The changes will come in proportion as we no longer feel that we alone are the elect but that at most we are the advance guard of all who do not know (or want to know) God, Christ, and Church, but who nevertheless do carry out what is in reality the essence of Christianity.

The opinion of Aquinas which we have just outlined is based on a transcendental analysis of the basic functions of mind or spirit (and in particular of those of willing and knowing). From the theological point of view, it has even greater probability. Behind the child stands the angel, who perpetually gazes on the face of God. Precisely because of its childhood, the child reaches into the sphere of the very grounds of the world. Now these are united by essential vision with the divinity and with the innermost reality of the cosmos. Consequently, the child walks serenely, without explicitly knowing it, over a triple abyss of reality, that of the angelic world and, consequently, of the universe, and over the abyss of the godhead.

To know a child, to be in reverent and loving association with him, therefore means opening oneself to the hidden abysses of reality, to what is promising and hopeful. Those who with respect and reserve protect a child, enabling him to prosper and develop, are in touch with all that is, and bring divine reality and a limitless future of hope into their own life.

Old People

The Bible testifies that those who are growing old stand in closer relation to divine things than anyone else. Consequently, they are a particular symbol of hope for the rest. A really wise old man makes an unforgettable impression. A few hours or a day or two are enough for one to fall under his spell. Not that he talks only of lofty and important things. It is his serene presence and detachment that transforms everything around him.

The old have this special power because they are not afraid any more (or ought not to be). They have reached the limit of achievement and success. They cannot add anything essential or lose what has been gained. Consequently, they are in a position to know by experience what really matters in life, and plumb its depths. It is also easier for them to forgive people and life generally. They are no longer trying to accomplish anything. Their life is no longer dominated by the drive and battle for mastery. For them it is more a question of power of endurance, of clear-sightedness about life, the strength of composure and inner lucidity. Their gentleness and benevolence are what strike and affect us irresistibly. We see a human being who wishes us well and who regards life and all its manifestations, and even the folly of the world, with goodwill. No one can lightly resist such simple goodness.

In *Le monde commence aujourd'hui,* Jacques Lusseyran describes various people he met in the Buchenwald concentration camp who helped him to overcome despair and meaninglessness. He describes with particular affection an old man, Jérémie Regard. Jérémie was a wise old man in the proper sense of the word, a cheerful old man. He died only a few weeks after Lusseyran's arrival in the camp, but made an unforgettable impression on him even in that short time. He spoke very little. He used merely to walk quietly through the huts, but transformed the whole situation by his serene presence. Not even he could give a meaning to the terrible events of concentration camp life, or in some

65

other way encourage others to endure. He was simply there, calm and cheerful. That was enough of a stimulus and inner support for everyone. Lusseyran describes how, when they saw him approaching, with his terrifying serenity and gaiety, they felt like shouting to him to open his eyes and see how atrocious everything around him was. But the words stuck in their throats, for he quite obviously saw all their misery, but quite unflinchingly. Moreover, he did not give the impression that it required an effort, that he was under strain, consciously heroic. He was simply not afraid, and that was just as natural to him as fear was to the rest.

Jérémie was obviously perfectly clear-sighted. He saw the horror on men's faces, staring in fascination at the smoke of the crematorium. He observed the quarrels among prisoners themselves, slowly mounting to hatred in the abominable atmosphere of terror. He saw men going mad; he saw the traitors. He missed nothing, but somehow or other his gaze pierced through everything and concentrated on something radiant yet quite matter of fact. But he disturbed no one by the intensity of his vision. He was not an emotional person. There was nothing unctuous about his gestures or the few things he did say. He was no prophet, simply a good man. His mere presence was what he had to give. Lusseyran says that he was like forgiveness there among them, a few steps from hell. For them it meant a new possibility, great happiness and enrichment.

What this man had achieved in life was transparency. Something absolute was revealed with radiant clarity through him. As Lusseyran puts it, he had plumbed his own depths and freed the essential, what does not depend on external circumstance at all, but is present everywhere and always, in sorrow and in joy. He had discovered the well-spring of life. The happiness he bore within himself so simply and naturally was not his alone, for he bestowed it liberally on all he met. His essential mystery was something other than his transitory and surface personality. It was the mystery of a hope so real that it gave him total detachment. Contact with such people shows what mature, unshakable hope really means.

It is a great misfortune for mankind that while there are certainly many aging human beings, there are but few who are genuinely old and wise like the one we have just described. Ronald Knox, writing when he himself was getting on in years, once lamented this tragedy of our time. He remarks bitterly, that we expect serenity and peace from the old, but instead they are touchy, irritable, and fussy, a constant burden to the patient relatives who look after them. Instead of being resigned and gradually retiring into the background, they want to dominate the conversation. They must have an audience for their anecdotes about the days when they were young. Instead of judging men and affairs indulgently, as one would expect from the experience of a long life, they are full of inveterate prejudices and critical of those they dislike. They cling to their privileges. One might have thought they would be above such trifles. They boast of past achievements, yet the approach of the judgment ought surely to humble them. They greedily cling to the few pleasures left to them, although they ought already to be detached from earthly pleasures. If, nevertheless, we do come across a mellow old person who suffuses us with hope by his simple goodness, we should accept this gift gratefully. And we should show particular regard for these rare people, who are witnesses to hope.

The Sick

The sick a sign of hope? Yes. By their very helplessness, the sick are in God's hand—whatever their own personal attitude to their

illness. God always listens to them. Not only their prayer, helplessly stammered in their sufferings, finds access to God, but the
suffering itself, their condition of sheer, radical helplessness, the
state of a creature left defenselessly to perish. What surrounds
them closest of all is God's loving mercy. Anyone who has
watched by the sick bed of a friend or someone they love, will
understand or catch at least a glimpse of what that means.

Our sick friend lay before us in heavy restless sleep. We dared
not move for fear he might waken. We sat motionless, holding in
our hands as it were our friend's tremulous life. Then we began
to bear his illness and pain ourselves, while he lay there and the
pain gradually ebbed from him. Our whole self went out to him.
The world shrank to the dimensions of a room where we bore the
pain of a friend and our own distress. By this utter devotion we
realized something that we have never dared or been able to explain properly to anyone, namely, that in our helpless human
devotion itself the infinity of the divine mercy was already present. Our own compassion made us know what God is, formed in
fact a proof by experience that a God of infinite mercy does exist.
The great question we had so often secretly put to ourselves and
vainly tried to answer: "If suffering exists, how can there be a
God?" was suddenly transformed into the question: "Could we
really apprehend God at all if our friend were not suffering there
in front of us?" Our silent sympathy suddenly became a revelation of God. Precisely because there could be no purely earthly
reply to our outcry, and because our mute love for this fellow
creature seemed humanly hopeless, they became an expression of
God's mercy. We realized with self-evident clarity that our lament
was not addressed to the void but to God.

This experience is so tenuous, belongs to such an extent to the
border regions of mysticism, that further rational analysis must

necessarily break down. Here we can only point to the direct character of the experience: Did we not—perhaps only unconsciously—utter the words of lament into a domain of divine mercy, which is invisibly and inseparably connected with our human helplessness?

Saint Augustine in his *Confessions* (I, 6) expresses this experience on one occasion as follows, "yet suffer me to speak, unto Thy mercy, me, dust and ashes. Yet suffer me to speak, since I speak to Thy mercy, and not to scornful man." We understand this as follows. Every great human action, all sympathy, all questioning and wrestling with meaning, origins, pain, and distress would inevitably seem odd if all there were were the world, humanity, and human things. From a purely terrestrial point of view we would at all times, everywhere, and in every respect be a metaphysical oddity. Precisely because we do not feel our sympathy and questioning outcry to be meaningless and odd, that is, do not feel them to be hopelessly shut in on themselves and addressed to no one, we know about God's mercy, even when we cannot name it. This profoundly human experience, difficult to express for that very reason, shows that as human beings we are at no point abandoned to absolute exteriority, but live totally and from the first within the domain of an interiority, in the love of God. To share the company and suffering of the sick can therefore become a place where God is revealed to us, and where hope is born.

In his *Meditations on the Psalms,* Gerhard Ebeling expressly points out that the power of evil would like to prevent our realizing the presence of God's mercy, by contesting our right to invoke God, and even by making this impossible. That is the main attack of the adversary, what makes the enemy an enemy. But what effect could this temptation have if the believer himself did not make room for it, if he did not have the enemy in his own heart, making common cause with the enemy outside, if our own heart were not continually telling us that we have no right to have recourse to God? Our heart keeps telling us we have no right to invoke God, that we are not worthy of his help, that we are in a prison quite shut off from the slightest noise from outside, that we can shout as much as we like, the sound will only re-echo from the cellar walls. There is no one to hear, it tells us, no answer, no hope, only comfortless loneliness; there is no help in God. This is how it becomes really clear what is the most radical kind of enmity we have to encounter. The power that deprives us of the right to hope and consequently of the courage to hope, and that makes us capitulate before the darkness, brings us to the point of passing sentence on ourselves and agreeing that "There is no help from God for him."

It is evident how vulnerable the immediate heartfelt sense of God's mercy is, which we have just described, how strongly we have to defend hope against our own heart, and, in order to cultivate our experience of hope, how often we have to counter-attack with the apparently paltry but victorious weapon of hope, with those simple words of which we must constantly remind ourselves, "God is greater than our hearts" (1 Jn. 3, 20).

The Presence of the Dead

In order to make clear to some degree the presence of the dead and their power to help, we have to start with quite simple everyday, matter-of-fact experiences. An example would be that of the remoteness of someone actually present and of the presence of someone far away. Persons may be in the room with us, so close that we could touch them. We see them, talk to them, ask questions which they answer, and they ask us questions. They are there. And yet perhaps we feel that, despite all our various points of contact, they are not really present; they do not really mean anything to us.

We may have the contrary experience. Someone else, a friend or other person dear to us who is on the other side of the globe, or already dead, is essentially closer to us than the human being who is in our room. It is one of the principal (but frequently neglected) functions of philosophy to reflect on such everyday experiences.

The very nature of love involves a statement that is made whenever and wherever love is felt: "For you I exist, I am there." This includes another statement, not so clear but no less real: "It is so true that I exist for you and in your eyes, that you cannot die, cannot wholly disappear from my presence." Perhaps unconsciously and without fully realizing the implications, every genuine lover affirms: "It is impossible for you not to be always with me. I myself, loving you as I do, would no longer exist if you no longer did. But I am alive and therefore so are you, even if you are far from me, even beyond the grave. I shall perhaps receive no sign of your presence. But between us there need be no sign and no verification. Nothing that happens to us can destroy this eternity inherent in our love. I should be consenting to your destruction and my own, denying the very nature of our love and, to the extent that it is in my power, I should be handing you over to eternal death, if I did not affirm with all the force of my very existence as a person that you will live on after death, whatever the superficial evidence to the contrary."

To some people these intimations of the presence of the dead in the love of the living may perhaps look like merely subjective

71

suasions. But precisely because of their subjectivity they possess a particularly effective concrete power to produce objective conviction. The experience we have just described belongs to the inner world of love. This sphere of knowledge has little to do with the "objective" and objectifiable knowledge based on measurements and logical conclusions which we employ every day. It is nonetheless a source of knowledge of reality.

The structure of this mode of knowledge which is subjective yet nevertheless truly penetrates into reality, might be outlined as follows. The lover sees himself and his own life as a shared life. In this way he recognizes the presence within him of his beloved who, moreover, is there as the ground and condition of his own self as lover. By this awareness, the reality of the other is posited and affirmed just as decisively as his own. This inner apprehension of the essence and destiny of another's reality has a structure which makes it possible for us, from our love of a dead person, to infer his presence and consequently his continued life, and to do so with the same certainty with which we experience and apprehend our own reality.

Immortality is therefore implied, co-posited, and affirmed in all genuine love. The experience of a personal relationship between a living person and someone whom they love but who is dead and whose being is hidden in mystery, throws light on the existence of both. This light of experience, this personally experienced certainty of the survival of the beloved, cannot be given objective expression. It is not observable or measurable. Nevertheless, it fills the soul of the person here on earth and forms the very basis of his life. The light shed on this world by the beloved dead gives the living a glimpse of the glory of a world to come; he becomes aware of his own hope, feels the closeness of God whose mercy and love surrounds the departed forever.

It is precisely the subjective character of the experience we have been describing, the impossibility of justifying it on extrinsic grounds, that constitutes its objectively demonstrative force. Of course, the experience itself remains inexplicable. In other words, we cannot trace it back to its constitutive elements, efficient causes and results, or only through subsequent reflection (immortality, resurrection, purgatory, judgment, hell, heaven, cosmic transformation, and so forth). Nevertheless, it can be made intelligible for oneself and even for others. Once experienced, it can be given a meaningful place in the structure of personal life and thus communicated to others, by inviting them to share the experience and join in philosophical reflection on it. It is a summons to them, a psychological stimulus to experience the same thing themselves and seriously to examine their own love for someone who is dead. All this awakens that unrest which prompts thoughtful consideration of the subjective states referred to, and leads to the real truth content of experience, thus transforming its intimations into explicitly conscious hope.

The Gentle

If we run over the main themes of our meditations so far, one persistent insight clearly dominates all the details: hope is found in giving hope to others; authentic humanity consists in dedication and detachment from self; the self is found in selflessness. We have therefore been attempting to describe a basic attitude which can enable us to come to know the silent mystery of God, even in a world of superficiality, struggle for power, and alienation. Deliverance can only come today from a fundamental change of direction. To put it in concrete terms, and perhaps a little harshly, we must be able to turn to what, by the standards of practical utility, leads nowhere and appears weak and quite inadequate in our world of ephemeral certainties. Thus, for example, we must learn to deal lovingly and devotedly with the weak and insignificant. We have to learn by experience the metaphysical force of children, the aged, the sick, and the dead. We have to inhabit in silence a world torn to pieces by talk.

Is hope an attitude of the weak? At first sight it might seem so. But nowadays we have to protect just such values as these, which are regarded as ineffectual but which are the profound justification and support of life against the attack of current everyday opinions. We have to combine them into a life-giving and world-transforming attitude.

It is in this connection that we want to point out the nature and power of Christian meekness. It is an extremely urgent task for Christians at the present time to think out the subject afresh, and its role as a testimony to hope. The early Christians realized the power of meekness, the sacred character and strength of defenselessness. A new force entered the world with the martyr who trembled but stood firm, not revolting against anyone, and not debasing his suffering by ill-will or vanity. It is a great good fortune to meet a truly gentle person; it can mark a whole life. Conviction of the high worth of defenselessness was never actually lost among Christians, but in the course of the centuries it was pushed out of the center of Christian thought. Our present situation in history, however, obliges all Christians to examine their attitude towards power and force in the light of the gospel. It is impossible for a Christian today to shut his eyes any longer to the scandal of violence. The plain truth of Christ's explicit teaching on non-violence is evident now with unparalleled clarity. Perhaps on this account, by this rediscovery of Christian meekness, we are at a turning point in Christian history; Christian spirituality is going to be substantially enriched. There are already Christians who are as ready and determined to practice non-violence as the Christians of the first few centuries were prepared for martyrdom.

The core of Christian meekness and gentleness is not an abstract statement or a particular attitude towards reality, but the person of Jesus Christ. Silent contemplation of Christ's gentleness alone can produce the growth in spiritual gentleness of character which is a specifically Christian vocation. The longer we meditate on the life of Christ, the more frequently we allow his mysterious power fully to influence us by daily consideration of his personal attitude and outlook, the more overwhelming the impression made by his almost disturbing gentleness. The outer appearances of mildness hide a perfect interior freedom, complete peace of mind. This man was so free that, unlike most people, he had no need of opposition and hostility to spur him on. In a world torn by hatred, total absence of hostility was achieved at last— in Christ.

His gentleness was always sensitive and receptive, and was able to produce truth where only confusion had prevailed before. For that quality does lead to a particular plenitude of truth. A human being who has achieved this kind of gentleness can perform even the slightest actions of his life in such a way that the people he is dealing with are awakened to their own latent existential truth. Above all, the truth that is rooted in gentleness is merciful. Our petty truths are so sharp-edged, simply because they are mere facets of truth, and ultimately spring from antagonism. The powerful, pacific, complete, and sensitive gentleness of Christ was a considerate, protective attitude to all reality, a readiness to offer shelter to others exposed and vulnerable. It was an attitude which refused from the start to harm anyone.

That is, of course, a negative account and does not make plain its positive side. This is in fact almost impossible to describe. Perhaps it is indicated in one of the oldest titles of honor applied to Christ, which Peter uses in his discourse to the people in the third chapter of Acts (3, 15). Still under the direct and powerful impact of Christ's presence, Peter calls Christ *archegos tes zoes,* the "prince of life," which can also mean the "author" and "leader" of life. The fullness of life, the energy of the living world, was concentrated in Christ. Nevertheless, this power, in him, was indescribably tender, delicate, and literally inoffensive. The transcendent power of God which maintains our creation in being and animates cosmic evolution, that increasingly intense urge to life, renounces, in Christ, any use of force. Only the inwardly strong can really be gentle. Our petty violence is masked by what are downright signs of weakness—our petty irritations, pretensions to superior insight, the perhaps unexpressed but quite obvious disapproval by which we persecute our fellow men, our virtuous indignation and petty humiliations. We squander the energy of our own heart, merely in order to inflict harm on others.

If we attempt to understand the gentleness of Christ's character, we notice the elemental force with which something inexpressible in human categories radiates from this man of Nazareth. We read, after all, "learn from me, for I am gentle" (Mt. 11, 29). This clearly states that the commandment of Christian gentleness is essentially an invitation to follow Christ; it cannot therefore be transformed forthwith into moral principles. Accordingly, we should not try to turn the gospel into a handbook of ethics or, still less, of casuistry. It describes an attitude which we shall never achieve in this life. Perhaps Christ was not primarily concerned with actual achievement at all. His aim was rather to encourage personal aspiration towards a general attitude of gentleness, to suggest vistas of possibility, lay down a progressive principle that would eventually produce a new world. Nearly all Christ's precepts and the demands of the Sermon on the Mount are of this kind, intended to point out a goal. It is very definitely open to doubt whether a Christian can renounce every use of force in the present interim period of the history of salvation between Christ's resurrection and second coming, in which a world transformed by holiness is already present but still has to coexist with godlessness, not merely in regard to external circumstances but even within the life of faith itself. Failure to see this argues ignorance of what is at stake in the world. Moreover, a closer look at so-called unconditional pacifists and advocates of non-violence shows that quite often they are very impatient, intolerant, and domineering. Meekness without detachment or discernment can become a terribly violent weapon, quite capable of driving fellow men to despair.

Our interpretation of Christian gentleness has emphasized its individual character as an individual vocation, so that it points in the direction of the evangelical counsels. But this does not lessen its universal validity and obligation in the slightest; it merely emphasizes that Christian gentleness is only attained through personal relations with a gentle God, with Christ. This also implies that the individual Christian must discover for himself the measure, kind, place, form, and quality of the gentleness which he personally has to achieve as his own individual witness. The obligation of gentleness depends on the intensity of the call which comes to him from Christ. At the same time, it must be emphasized that this vocation, which is addressed to every Christian, but only recognized and accepted through a personal relationship with Christ, is heard by a wider and wider range of Christians today.

This process would seem to show (though this is obviously difficult to prove) that individuals are converging towards a new historical state of the world. The evolution of the universe is leading to a new pattern of reality, still distant, perhaps, hidden and obscure, almost imperceptible, yet continually and decisively gaining in clarity and effectiveness, one of gentleness. An extraordinary mutation is taking place in that evolution. Christians have the obligation—because it is part of the very spirit and outlook of the gospel—to believe unreservedly in the possibility and necessity of the universal gentleness (or friendliness) which appeared among us and radiated from the face of Christ, and to bear witness in that way to a new hope for mankind.

What is in question is an attitude of inner readiness not to parry blows with blows, the attitude of the martyr. Many of them adopted the attitude of absolute meekness in their sufferings. In fact that is precisely what made them martyrs. They were following Paul's advice, living the "very short" remnant of their life in this world "as though they had no dealings with it" (cf. 1 Cor. 7, 29-31). This attitude made them prophets, because they testified how the gentleness of God's love can be announced by an actual life in which all self-seeking is transcended. The attitude of the martyr reveals a world to come. Martyrdom (whether of blood or the daily round) is the point in reality at which a world of darkness waits expectantly for light and bears witness to the actual existence of this light. This shows the eschatological character of Christian meekness, which bears witness to the future state of the universe, by pointing forward to a transfigured, because gentle and non-violent, world.

The Silent

Silence is not an incidental feature of authentic human existence, it is the very foundation of the interior life. Werner Bergengruen's poem "O come, power of silence" is not only a reflection on our present condition but also a guide and refuge: "We are so betrayed, destitute of all consolation. In all the shrill deeds there is nothing that frees us. We are weary of hints and coarse remarks. We want the sound of the silence that created us. The power, greed, and will of noisy people die away. Come, power of silence and transform the world." External silence is merely the expression of an inner state. Speech has to be renounced inwardly, if depth and plenitude are to emerge from what we are. Silence is the way in which life grows towards its goal. In silence man is able to live close to things as they really are, truly to inhabit the earth. What does this mean? We shall point to four essential features of silence.

In silence the world becomes man's dwelling place in the full sense. Silence creates a home and native place. First of all, through salvage operations, the essential is safely disentangled. It is also where human existence finds a firm foundation. Silence, therefore, means distinguishing essential knowledge acquired through experience in the course of life from its context of chance and daily routine, thus preventing its being overborne by the momentary and superficial. Silence therefore makes it possible for us to get close to our own selves, consider the moments in which we have most clearly experienced the reality of things, people, and events, and assimilate them into ourselves. This salvages what is illuminating and meaningful in everyday life. In this sense, silence is also poetry.

Our everyday existence is described by Martin Heidegger by the term "chatter." He sees this as a threat to our authentic life. We are mere chatter because we can never express our whole reality in its entirety. And the reason we cannot do so is that we "are" not yet. We never fully possess and know our own reality; we ex-sist—we are not identical with ourselves, still unrealized. We cannot put ourselves wholly into our action at any particular moment. The opacity and inexpressibility of our human reality is due to what we call "temporality." Our being is fragmented in time in the form of experiences of differing degrees of intensity. Only occasionally, in moments of mental intensity, do we succeed in encountering and penetrating the essential in things, and so come face to face with ourselves. Otherwise our actions are merely a vain pursuit of ourselves from moment to moment.

This structure of our human reality (of our earthly lingering among things and persons, among our own experiences) is known to the theological view of man as "concupiscence." This denotes the impossibility of complete personal mastery of our own reality during our earthly life. On the plane of knowledge of God, this also involves a radical inability to attain God. We only come in contact with "reality" at a few points in the course of life. Usually we enter unawares into the splendid landscape of existence. Apprehension of meaning is also fragmentary and divided up among various unrelated moments in the flow of our personal life. It is never more than an unexpected and incalculable flash of enlightenment as to what we are living through. We grope forward uncertainly into the fog of our projects and intentions. To preserve the lucid, transparent moments of our life, to recognize their meaning and lessons, to link them anew and creatively, thus bringing about a different and significant relation between one's own life and the world, is essentially the work of silent reflection. Silence produces interior unity.

A world arises in this way which is not only more beautiful, more living, and deeper than the domain of our daily round, but points beyond it to something transcendent. From mosaic tesserae of our scattered insights into the meaning of the world, meditative silence builds a home of light and space. A domain at the heart of things opens out and foreshadows the indescribable reality which revelation calls "the new heaven and the new earth." To inhabit the world in silence, therefore, means to make the meaning of the world one's own, by coming to know it by experience and participation. It means allowing what is essential in things to reach us, to look back with warm memories of the radiant experiences of one's life, and to establish a new relation to the world on this basis. How is this done?

Aquinas draws attention to a significant fact of experience recorded in scripture: "The heart of the wise is where there is mourning; and the heart of fools where there is mirth" (Eccles. 7, 5; *Summa theologica,* 2a, 2ae, q. 114, a. 1 ad 3). A remarkable text! Similarly Martin Heidegger in his interpretation of a posthumous poem by Georg Trakl, "Lend your flame to the spirit, ardent melancholy," emphasizes that meditative silence is a painful experience, only achieved when the soul "flares up" under the influence of melancholy. "The spirit," says Heidegger, "is flame. Red-hot, it gives light. The light is in the contemplative gaze. To such contemplation there comes the reality of what is manifested, in which all that is essentially real inheres. This ardent contemplation is grief. Its essence is closed to any thinking that imagines grief on the basis of sensation. Ardent contemplation is proportionate to the greatness of the soul."

In these texts, melancholy is described as a fundamental condition or even as the chief factor of silence. It has, of course, nothing to do with sentimentality and luxuriant self-indulgence in feelings of mental depression. It means, rather, a habitual awareness of the gravity or high seriousness of personal life. This in turn is simply the realization of the significance of reality, prompted by personal contact with surpassing excellence, as a result of which man is conscious that access to this excellence is still barred to him. He is perpetually turned back into the commonplace here and now. He has become a stranger, banished from two worlds. Encounter with what is of surpassing excellence has made the world of here and now seem empty to him, and robbed of all its magic the world landscape as he used to see it. At the same time, however, the surpassingly excellent has remained beyond the reach of the soul, incomprehensible, mysteriously withdrawn. This experience of the human condition on the boundary is what we are calling melancholy, gravity, that *grande tristezza* of which Dante speaks, man's disquiet at the simultaneous presence and absence of God.

Silence is a leave-taking. Gravity concentrates the mind in detachment. And the mind always involves separation. Everywhere it creates distance, precisely by becoming aware of things. The "intelligible presence" of things to the mind is constituted by a combination of proximity and distance.

In *Menon's Lament for Diotima,* Hölderlin writes: "Something friendly from afar must be close to me." This is the element which gives our experiences their intellectual character. We only exist as mind and spirit in virtue of this dialectic. Each disclosure only uncovers the presence of something further hidden. What the mind grasps always ultimately displays itself to us as profoundly mysterious, withdrawn, inaccessible. Throughout the history of Israel, we meet with the same structure in revelation; God's close presence is disclosed, but as insuperably transcendent. Reserve, non-manifestation, is inherent in the disclosure made in revelation, just as it is in all love and friendship. The two movements—disclosure and non-manifestation—are complementary; they even constitute the essence of our spiritual nature. The fundamental experience of the mind is that of the presence of the incomprehensible.

If this awareness of simultaneous presence yet remoteness of incomprehensible meaning is achieved as a habitual attitude towards reality, that is, as a virtue, silence is the result. Not merely absence of speech, parsimony of actions, spatial seclusion, but something more positive, an essential detachment in which even the slightest things can become endlessly significant, disclosing what they hold in reserve, what they tacitly imply. Such detachment is perhaps already an anticipation of that radical close presence to the world which happens in the moment of death. In this perspective of detachment as a means of perceptive awareness it might perhaps be possible to work out convincingly a theology of the Christian counsels, of the obligations imposed by the Sermon on the Mount, of the contemplative life, and also of death.

To sum up. The Christian is, in Paul's words, an "envoy of hope." He encounters that hope in inconspicuous places, in a child, an old man, the dead, in gentle, or silent people. That was the revolutionary alteration of all our ideas which Christ brought us. Greatness and hope only fall to the share of those who selflessly go out among the "little ones."

The picture of man that we have referred to and attempted to sketch in these first three meditations is in itself sublime, beautiful, and true. It shows man as essentially an embodiment of hope, a dreamer, gazing into the future which is his own hidden self; it presents him as bearing witness to hope. But is that really what we are in fact? Are we that kind of people already? There are moments in life when man does appear noble, great, and full of hope. But then things become painful and hard again, everything about the human heart seems repulsive and petty. What was God's real idea in creating man? What does he himself think of his handiwork? Was it an attempt that failed? No. There are people whose aspiration is as it should be. They are attractively full of life. They are young and fresh in outlook, forward-looking in far-reaching ways, gifted with an unfailing feeling for greatness. They have experienced for themselves what the psalmist described, "The Lord was my stay. He brought me forth into a broad place . . . because he delighted in me" (Ps. 18, 19–20). If we meet such people, we see at once what a human being can be and why God loves him so much. But how does one become a person of that kind? The next meditation will attempt to outline an answer to the question.

4

The Central Question
of Hope

In this meditation we want to risk a decisive step in the direction of a spirituality inspired by hope. The basic claim will be that Christian holiness consists in bearing witness to heaven by our life on earth. John sums up the structure of a developing personal life as follows: "Beloved, we are God's children now; it does not yet appear what we shall be, but we know that we shall be like him, for we shall see him as he is. And everyone who thus hopes in him, purifies himself as he is pure" (1 Jn. 3, 2-3).

The dialectic contained in this statement is remarkable, for despite its simplicity it comprises the whole mystery of the Christian practice of hope. It says we already know the essential, the one thing necessary. Even more, as children of God we already bear within us an essential kinship with God as the ontological ground of our life as persons. On the other hand, this knowledge and being includes what we do not know and what we are not yet. Our eternal reality is not yet manifest, because God has not yet fully appeared. The manifestation of God will bring to man a supreme and ultimate knowledge of God, and this in turn will produce a new entitative resemblance to God in man. Until then, man has to hope. Hope has its place in the domain of tension between not-knowing and not-yet-being on the one hand, and knowledge and actual being on the other. Its inherent tendency is to enter the earthly domain in order to bear witness to heaven. Now concrete testimony to heaven constitutes Christian holiness. Consequently, the question of holiness is the central problem of hope. But what is Christian holiness?

Christian life has to be understood as essentially the process by which heaven comes about. In order to know what Christian holiness consists in, therefore, we must project the structure of heaven back into the activities of earthly life. This is the only way we can form some idea of the pattern of Christian holiness. That is what will be attempted here.

Heaven Is Perfect Fulfillment

We are twice born into life, once when we leave our mother's womb and a second time when we are delivered from that of the world—in other words, at birth and at death.

At birth, a frail being is exposed to total disaster. All at once the protective and sheltering home of the mother's womb is no longer there. The child is forcibly expelled, and for the first time it utters the cry of the creature in danger of perishing. At the same time, a wonderful transformation takes place in its relation to the world. A new world gradually opens out before the small human creature. Light shines on its darkness, colors glow before its eyes, tender hands calm its fears, love surrounds its whole being.

In death, something of the same kind takes place, only in a much more radical way. Once again man is forced out of his narrow limits. The whole human being collapses, because the worldly domain which until then has afforded him a home in body and soul is taken from him. At the same time, however, a new dimension of the cosmos opens out before him. Man goes down to the very ground of the world, becomes totally present in the cosmos. His soul is freed from its limitation by impenetrable circumstances, and is placed in a cosmos transparent to God and in a transfigured body.

We know almost as little of what happens in this process, and therefore of what heaven is, as the child in its mother's womb knows about the world. Heaven transcends our thoughts to such an extent that practically all we can say about it is what it is not. Only enough was revealed to us about heaven for us not to grow weary of waiting. One thing at least we do know with certainty—heaven is perfect fulfillment and boundless happiness. As such it is the focus and acme of all that as human beings we can imagine and desire. Accordingly, if we are to say what heaven is, we must decide in what direction our life spontaneously seeks its perfect fulfillment. We must then extend that line to infinity, into limitless happiness. That will give a distant glimpse of heaven. What are the essential directions of human fulfillment? We shall pick out three

Structures of Human Fulfillment

Our first thesis concerns the fundamental aspiration that inspires every human being, even if it does not emerge explicitly into reflective consciousness. It runs as follows.

Human Life Attains Fulfillment in Poverty

Superficial experience appears to teach just the opposite. Life is perfected by possession. Man is in various respects a deficient being. His vital powers are not sufficient to defend him in the world in which the will of his creator has placed him. From the purely biological point of view he would perish if he did not possess another power. He is able to gain mastery over the earth. He surrounds himself with a protective shell, makes the cosmic energies serve him, thus creating a new world between himself and the world. He does not adapt himself to the world; he transforms the world into an artificial sphere in which he can live despite his own inadaptation. By mastering the world he escapes the conditions imposed by environment. Possession, world-mastery, property, and dominion are therefore forms of human fulfillment, and man could not exist at all without them.

Why do we maintain all the same that human life attains fulfillment in poverty? Because the human drive to possession must necessarily be transformed into poverty. The impulse to possession essentially impels us to share in reality other than our own. But the higher a reality stands in the hierarchy of being, the less it can be possessed. The highest values, love, for example, cannot be coerced, cannot be conquered by the means that serve to master the world. If we are to share in some other person's being, we must set them free, renounce any attempt to treat them as property. In other words, we must adopt an attitude of poverty. The highest wealth, participation in God, is sheer grace. God's grace is something totally incalculable, which contradicts all presuppositions and conjectures. God gives his presence where and when he wills. Nothing is given to man by God which would be his in any case. God's coming is something that befalls man. Ultimately, man can (and need) do nothing except allow himself in silent surrender to be enriched. Human fulfillment is a gift bestowed. We are always poor in that respect. The opener the attitude we maintain, the more receptive, that is, unfulfilled, we are, the more we can receive as gift, the more perfect the accomplishment that awaits us. And even the ability to remain receptive, the capacity to create a void of poverty within us which can be filled, is itself a gift bestowed on us. In the most essential respects man has hope of fulfillment only if he be "poor." Our second principle therefore affirms:

Human Life Attains Fulfillment in Chastity

Here, too, the contrary appears to be the case. After all, life seeks completion in the direction of love. Without this it would be impossible to attain the indispensable insight which inspires the attitude of spiritual poverty, the realization that our self is fulfilled in self-surrender. For love is, of course, precisely and essentially a surrender of self. It is a totally disinterested affirmation of another's reality, with consequent confirmation of our own existence as a person, total self-giving, and receiving. One essential form of it, which for many is their God-given life's task and way of fulfillment, is the spiritual love which is given the bodily expression in which life is created anew, becomes one with itself again, and produces a new being other than itself.

Nevertheless, bodily love itself leads to chastity. Genuine love demands more than bodily contact. It expresses unconditional affirmation of the beloved partner; it would not wish to make use of, or make demands on, the beloved, but only seeks his well-being, seeks to show tenderness, not to make claims. Ardent love becomes an unmixed affirmation of the beloved who, precisely because he is loved, cannot be treated as a possession. This ardent and loving presence, unalloyed self-giving, unconditional devotion, is chastity. By attaining its perfection, love can be transformed into an essential chastity, a kind of virginity. Our third and last thesis is that:

Human Life Attains Fulfillment in Obedience

The perfection of life lies in the direction of ever greater freedom. First, in increasing liberation from the immediacy of the instincts, but also, and above all, in increasingly effective self-determination. Finally, there is a third factor which is really the most essential—the possibility of freely binding oneself. Man is only free in the true sense if he becomes so independent that he no longer clings to himself and seeks his own satisfaction and fulfillment, but what brings happiness and advantage to others.

This ecstatic, fully achieved freedom finds realization in obedience, when freedom wills nothing except to serve, to be put to use. Here a man gives his heart away, self-effacingly, unselfishly. Such freedom is the spontaneous love and energy of a heart moved by goodness. There is a profoundly tender regard for reality in freedom of this kind, an absence of calculation, a willingness, readiness, and receptivity for what is new. The soul is evidently still fresh and capable of advancing towards greater fulfillment; it sets no obstacle to the coming of greater things. This is youthfulness of spirit with its joyous and flexible character. Such freedom says Yes to all that is, addresses every being with love: sister sun, brother fire, brother death, and brother man. It wills to be obedient to them, that is to say, to recognize and acknowledge them in their own essential reality.

Above all, however, obedient freedom of this kind sets God free to act, as it were, gives him a handle for his action. God's life, which lies deeper than man's deepest depths, can now make itself felt in him. If our existence shuts itself off, God is tied, but if it opens itself, a new expanse appears which God's reality can enter and where a second creation, the new creation, begins. This is the miracle which Jesus intended to announce above all, the miracle of the coming of a new world. Our conclusion is therefore:

Fulfillment Is Achieved in the Loving Gift of Self

If life is essentially perfected in poverty, chastity, and obedience, it is impossible to enter heaven without them. Death will give all of us the possibility of freely achieving utter poverty and chastity and unconditional obedience. Only if man brings himself to nothing (accepts his poverty which is at the same time total receptivity), if he dedicates his own being unreservedly (achieves his chastity by total reserve) and gives himself without calculation (affirms his obedience with the ultimate unconditionality of his own freedom), can he enter into perfect fulfillment. In this sense the gospel demands of poverty, chastity, and obedience apply to every Christian and admit of no exception.

Heaven therefore consists in a total poverty. The limits of our being are broken down to make us open to an infinite fulfillment, a fulfillment which itself creates a continual capacity for the even greater fulfillment that ensues. Heaven also consists in an unconditional chastity. There we are devoted to others, sensitive to them, giving ourselves without expectation of return. Our poverty will give us strength for this. Finally, heaven consists in unconditional obedience. Our very being will form a Yes of consent to infinity, to a limitless perfection which fulfills us more and more as it disposes over us. We will willingly enter into what is always other than ourselves. Our chastity will make us capable of this.

It is clear that poverty, chastity, and obedience are not three different virtues but the single quality of a love which is a self-giving and has achieved absolute fulfillment precisely in self-giving. These considerations also show that poverty, chastity, and obedience are not an exceptional choice reserved only to a few, but are the fundamental law of the new creation. Every Christian must realize them in his life, or at least in death.

Attainment of Holiness

Bearing witness is something that belongs to revelation. By it, the inaccessible enters the world of the senses, becomes tangible and concrete in an actual human life. In the testimony to heaven, heaven itself is embodied. It becomes unmistakably plain that heaven exists, that it has power over a human being whose heart it can already fill to the full. The world we directly experience is still opaque in regard to heaven. Only in testimony does the world acquire a new transparency. A witness is like a crack that breaks through our world, through which the light of heaven shines. To be a witness it is, therefore, not enough for someone to be believing, pious, a man of interior life, well-informed about religious matters. He has to be profoundly affected by the reality of heaven if his life is to be radiant with it.

A person whose very being is actually affected by heaven through poverty, chastity, and obedience, is the summit of the universe and the fine flower of creation. Our world attains its perfection in him. He is the spearhead of cosmic development. Such a life is not in any way a denial of the world, but expresses deep love for our earthly nature. Nowhere else, in fact, is such love so radically expressed.

A desire, or even a thirst, for great things is evident in people today. Something unparalleled is emerging in human consciousness, a new aspiration, a new youthfulness of spirit, a new desire to break the existing framework of things, a new capacity for self-projection into the imagined future. Christianity will not hinder this new departure. Quite the opposite. It lights the way. Christ is the fulfillment of all aspirations. Everything that strives upwards is seeking the Lord. Christ stands at the very heart and center of all humanity's dreams. The risen Christ is a guarantee that no hope will remain unfulfilled, that none of our longings is lost in the void. Nowhere is the world so radically affirmed as in Christianity. This radical affirmation is what should be manifest in those human beings who have consecrated themselves by poverty, chastity, and obedience to heaven, the ultimate, infinitely perfect fulfillment of the world.

World-Affirmation

A human being who has attained interior freedom by spiritual poverty has a message for the world, not actually expressed in words, perhaps, but by the life he leads: "If one is to make progress it is not enough to be rich. You are too concerned about your security. You have to provide for your family. You have to see that you and yours do not suffer want. Our Lord has asked that of you, and you do well to make every effort to meet this demand. But you must not bind your heart, otherwise you and your world will not achieve fulfillment; you will not help the world forward or make a new world out of it.

Our Lord himself said how difficult it is for those who put their trust in riches to enter the kingdom of God. By this he meant precisely what you keep telling yourself in moments of insight: "I must break free; I must not shut myself up in what has already happened; I must go forward to new achievement; I must constantly fight against my own tendency to superficiality; I must not become a has-been, for what I really am lies in front of me; I cannot rest content, otherwise I shall not achieve anything, nothing will come of my dreams and my longing." Our Lord certainly does require you to be open and receptive to what is new; not to be entirely preoccupied in caring for your own; to make room within you for other things and other human beings; not to take yourself too seriously; to feel for the misfortunes of others; not to push yourself forward but let others have their place; not to seek continual confirmation of your own importance, but to concern yourself with the halt and blind; to feed the hungry; to give drink to the thirsty; to shelter strangers; to clothe the naked; to visit those in prison; to comfort those who mourn: in short, not to abandon the world but to show it that there is still hope for it.

That is the interior poverty of which our Lord spoke so earnestly. You will not find true joy anywhere else. It will not give you comfort, easy pleasure, gay frivolity. But there is deep joy in welcoming and caring for those the Lord sends. A man of interior poverty, that is, who does not put his trust in what has been achieved already, stands in sovereign independence of things. He uses them, because God has given them. But he uses them not out of mere avidity to have them but in order to care for those entrusted to him. He possesses things only to maintain a generous and cordial love. Do you think things will slip away from you if you do not cling to them? Not at all. A man possesses things in the truest sense only if he transforms them, assimilates their beauty, advances, by means of what they are, to their eternal ground. What familiarity with the things of this world is evident in parables of Jesus, yet he himself had nowhere to lay his head. Water, bread, gate, path, light, the whole world, in fact, are full of mystery in Jesus' parables, full of God's mystery which shines through even the most ordinary everyday things. Have no fear, then. You become richer, not by getting your hands on things but by understanding them. Do not let yourself be dominated, do not be satiated. Admit longing into your heart; be a human being who looks for even greater fulfillment. If you do not do this, life will wither in you and hope will die. You will not promote life; you will fetter and hold back humanity, which is everywhere dreaming of fulfillment and wants to step forward to a nobler future. If you really love the world, be poor in spirit!

This preaching of poverty will only be convincing, however, if the human witnesses to the greatness of poverty demonstrate to the world that the world itself can only be really loved in spiritual poverty. This ought not to be too difficult in itself. Those who are called "children of this world" know very well that every great work involves renunciation, that every achievement in the world demands effort, victory over inertia, over one's own self-satisfaction, that is to say, detachment is essential. How much peace and quiet men sacrifice every day to get on in the world. What a lot of himself a man loses in working for this earth. He has continually to tear himself away from himself. He knows very well what sacrifice is. The demand for detachment culminates in the Christian.

The Christian seeks God in all things. He no longer counts in his own eyes. He has completely forgotten himself. Consequently, the Christian *could* be the most detached of men and work in the purest and most unselfish way to serve a world developing towards the divine. He could radically humble himself, forget himself, that is, be poor in spirit. People would see that he had sacrificed himself defenselessly and unquestioningly, lost himself in others, that he is not seeking his own advantage, that he is an open-hearted and complete human being. Who could give himself more radically than the Christian, whose life after all consists in imitating his redeemer?

This mode of existence, the mind of Christ, is described in the Letter to the Philippians: "Have this mind among yourselves, which was in Christ Jesus, who, though he was in the form of God, did not count equality with God a thing to be grasped, but emptied himself, taking the form of a servant, being born in the likeness of men. And being found in human form, he humbled himself" (Phil. 2, 5–8). That is the only kind of disposition in which a man can be creative at all. And that is the Christian mentality. The witness to heaven should demonstrate concretely to the world of today that anyone who really loves the earth must love it in the Christian way. The Christian is not a tired member of the human race. He is not less but more a human being than the rest. "Are they Hebrews? So am I. Are they Israelites? So am I. Are they descendants of Abraham? So am I . . . I am a better one!" says Paul (2 Cor. 11, 22–23). We could add, "Are they human beings? I am even more of one." This *Plus et ago* ("I am even more") is precisely the point at which Christian witness today can begin. It shows that we are not poor because we have failed in the struggle for life, or because we expect an individual reward in heaven, but because we have realized that poverty is the way to the collective success of the world. We are not poor against the world but for the world.

Affirmation of Life

Chastity is not a negative quality. On the contrary, it is an undivided, wholly practical affirmation of life. The witness to heaven renounces a fulfillment of desire, not because he despises love but because he wants to give himself undividedly, and because his love carries him beyond any possibility of fulfillment. He wants to be able to devote himself to all, especially to those whom no one loves, who have never known what love is. Chastity is, therefore, essentially a positive assertion of life; it is simply that unconditional singleness of outlook which in the New Testament is called "simplicity of heart": total self-dedication. In other words, it is the state in which a man's heart is truly one and undivided, totally devoted, wholly in service, perfectly sincere. Such undivided devotion makes a human being radiant with the light of holiness. Purity is the habitual attitude of those who seek God "urgently," with every fiber of their being.

Holy scripture also uses the word *hagnotes* for this radiant manner of being. It is difficult to translate. It means more than simply purity; it includes holiness and wholeness, the inward radiance of a being who lives unconditionally for the unconditional, for God. In Christ, reality was radiantly transfigured. John reports on this vision of Christ: "Then I turned to see the voice that was speaking to me, and on turning I saw seven golden lampstands, and in the midst of the lampstands one like a son of man, clothed with a long robe and with a golden girdle round his breast; his head and his hair were white as white wool, white as snow; his eyes were like a flame of fire, his feet were like burnished bronze, refined as in a furnace, and his voice was like the sound of many waters; in his right hand he held seven stars, from his mouth issued a sharp two-edged sword, and his face was like the sun shining in full strength. When I saw him, I fell at his feet as though dead. But he laid his right hand upon me, saying, 'Fear not, I am the first and the last, and the living one; I died, and behold I am alive forever more ...'" (Rev. 1, 12–18). A message of life. The purest life overcame death and gave life its very vitality.

It is the task of Christians to bear witness to this vitality. They have to show the world this power of purity which promotes what is divine in us. Those who bear witness to heaven cannot be petty, must not give the impression that they love God because they cannot love anyone else, that they are seeking the eternal because they have no courage for the temporal. They must be transparently full of vitality in the world. Life must shine forth in them. The Acts of the Apostles testify that this can happen not only in Christ but in those who have dedicated themselves completely to Christ, when it is said of the deacon Stephen: "And gazing at him, all who sat in the council saw that his face was like the face of an angel" (Acts 6, 15).

Affirmation of Freedom

Christ embodied the attitude to life which is faintly foreshadowed in the psalm: "O Lord, my heart is not lifted up, my eyes are not raised too high; ... But I have calmed and quieted my soul, like a child quieted at its mother's breast; like a child that is quieted is my soul" (Ps. 131, 1–2). He gave himself as a human being completely into the hands of him who respects our freedom as no one else does, because he himself created that freedom. He submitted totally to the will of God which pervades the creation, drives it ever onwards and leads it towards a total liberation, heaven. He has accordingly become the spearhead of cosmic development: "...he became obedient unto death, even death on a cross. Therefore God has highly exalted him and bestowed on him the name which is above every name, that at the name of Jesus every knee should bow, in heaven and on earth and under the earth, and every tongue confess that Jesus Christ is Lord..." (Phil. 2, 8–11).

Our freedom consists in obeying him who has called us to freedom, who has brought milliards of freedoms into existence and wills to lead all of them to their perfection. If we submit to this creative power, we advance the world further towards its eternal destination. We do not lose our freedom by it. God's creative act does not coerce; on the contrary, it is exercised with great reserve. God creates us by making room for us, withdrawing, so to speak, his omnipotence and omnipresent being so that we may exist. And afterwards, when he has endowed us with a heart, he comes forward and appeals to us, saying with shattering urgency: "My son, give me your heart" (Prov. 23, 26; cf. 1 Chron. 28, 9). He tells us that, if we are willing, he will free us from our narrow limits and lead us into eternity, where we shall be perpetually renewed and experience perpetual transformation. But he will not compel us; we must do this freely. We are free, but our freedom is perfected by giving it to God. He can make the new creation only with our cooperation. Heaven comes to be by our making room for God in ourselves.

Every Christian who lives his Christianity honestly is called to this obedience. Every Christian has to keep himself receptive to God's guidance at every moment, since God makes known his will through the multiplicity of events, speaks to us through the course of history, through our situation at the moment, the chance occurrences of every day.

By obedience, the Christian, however, advances another step

into God's will. He asks a human being who is just as exposed to error and darkness as he is to tell him what God wants of him. By daring to make this total dedication, which God cannot answer except by turning to him with even more loving guidance, he brings God even more into the world. By his unconditional trust, he compels God to take him even more firmly by the hand. This ought not to be forgotten, especially by religious superiors. They do not represent God's guidance because they are particularly wise, gifted, or holy, but because their subjects have shown such great confidence in God that God simply cannot but bestow his special presence on the person who represents his providence, and reveal his will to him.

The Lord is not close to the world if this bond of obedience does not result in joy and freedom. Every time our Lord approached people after his resurrection, he said, "It is I. Fear not." Joy and fearlessness ought, therefore, to be a sign that human beings have entered upon fulfillment and are fully at one with the will of him who brings the world to its goal.

Those who bear witness to heaven do not obey because they are too weak to exercise their freedom, but because they desire even more freedom. They know that by abandoning themselves to God they give the world even more of God. The more obedience there is in the world, the more and the quicker God can transform it into heaven. Here is Mary's Yes, her free consent to total self-dedication, by which she gave the world the possibility of uniting itself with its creator and of blossoming into perfection.

In this way, the atmosphere surrounding these witnesses to heaven becomes increasingly radiant and charged with God. The ardent testimony of a life of poverty, chastity, and obedience brings a concentration of the divine in the world. An immeasurable force is concealed in it, the power of the divine presence in the world. The Christian is not something separate from the world. His very election in fact gives him solidarity with all mankind. The world has sent him on ahead so that he may prepare the way for mankind. He takes the life of the world with him into the breathtaking adventure of union with God. He has to draw others after him. A heavy responsibility rests on him, for he no longer belongs to himself but to mankind. He is God's gift to the world.

Poverty, chastity, and obedience mean maintaining a transparent unalloyed quality and disinterestedness in the world by uttermost personal effort. They require distinction of outlook, thought, and human relationships, a life radiating kindness and bringing hope, without much talk or feverish activity. This clears a space round them for other people to flourish, without threat, duly acknowledged and honored. The nobility of a life of poverty, chastity, and obedience demonstrates that reality can be fully respected and honored by a human being and treated with disinterested friendship; in other words, that there is still hope.

In human beings of this kind we realize that God as hope is really among us. But such people have often had to endure the most terrible loneliness in this world, in order to be able to fight their way to their utter authenticity. In the next meditation we wish to speak of their interior conquest of hope, their wrestling with God. Our hope has thus to be purified in the pain of experiencing the presence of God, the pain that grips us as we realize, "Lord I am not worthy."

5

Experience of Hope

The grandeur and distress of Christian life are described by Paul in the following words: "...in this world of [time], we live awaiting our blessed hope, the appearing of the glory of our great God" (Tit. 2, 12–13). A concrete theology of hope known by living experience finds concentrated expression here. Basic Christian insights appear in words that interpret human existence: "great God," "the appearing of God," "awaiting," "in this world," "blessedness." Human hope figures in this domain of experience. The fundamental polarity of the statement derives, however, from the contrasted terms "live in this world" and "great God." This calls for careful consideration.

Something overwhelming appears in the context of temporal circumstance and everyday trivialities: the "great God." By this manifestation man feels threatened and overtaxed. In the half-light of his temporal existence man never catches sight of God's countenance except as distorted in broken reflections. His relationship to the Absolute appears uncertain, unreal, and unstable to him. God cannot become undividedly "present" for him during his temporal existence. Man in relation to God "is" not yet in the proper sense of the word, he simply "ex-sists." In other words, he lives in a perpetual exteriority, always "already ahead of him-

ings who tried to carry out these precepts in their lives it is said: "They were stoned, they were sawn in two, they were killed with the sword; they went about in skins of sheep and goats, destitute, afflicted, ill-treated—of whom the world was not worthy..." (Heb. 11, 37-38). Even more insistently, "in toil and hardship, through many a sleepless night, in hunger and thirst, often without food, in cold and exposure. And apart from other things, there is the daily pressure upon me of my anxiety..." (2 Cor. 11, 27-28). That was the kind of life they led. Finally, it is even suggested that man has not fully met the demands of this love until in the battle against his inner disintegration he has "resisted to the point of shedding his blood" (Heb. 12, 4). Here, martyrdom—whether that of blood or of the fulfillment of daily duties—is made the criterion of faith and love.

To throw light on these themes, the theological reflection of Thomas Aquinas is of great importance. In his spiritual writings, above all in *De perfectione vitae spiritualis* (1269) and the *Contra retrahentes homines a religionis ingressu* (1271), as well as in the relevant sections of the *Summa theologica* (especially 2a, 2ae, q. 184 and 186), he opposes the view that the endeavor to achieve boundless love of God is reserved for a few and cannot therefore be regarded as a universal requirement of the love of God as such. By a precise though phenomenologically not very elaborate analysis of human love, he shows that love is always a total self-giving; any half-heartedness and reserve destroys its authenticity. Man is dynamically limitless. In decisive and ultimate respects, human aspiration knows no limits. Any limitation imposed on the human impulse to love ultimately destroys the life of the human person.

The Christian precept of love brings this open dynamism of the human mind to fulfillment; love itself constitutes "religion":

105

"You, therefore, must be perfect, as your heavenly Father is perfect" (Mt. 5, 48). This love which strives after God's perfection is proved in earthly life by willingness to "lay down our lives" (1 Jn. 3, 16), and by cultivation of an attitude towards one's brethren which "bears all things, believes all things, hopes all things, endures all things" (1 Cor. 13, 7). And Christ himself confirms and repeats the original commandment of this relationship to God and makes it the criterion of holiness: "You shall love the Lord your God with all your heart, and with all your soul, and with all your mind" (Mt. 22, 37).

On the plane of practical conduct of life, however, all this inevitably means human failure. As a consequence, man is thrown into uncertainty and darkness. For the greater God becomes for him, the more unbridgeable the gulf which separates him from communion with God will inevitably appear. But God's very remoteness will impel a heart that has once taken fire to set off on its search again and again. Each time it is a harsh necessity, and means taking leave of familiar, favorite things and events, desires and plans. And in every respect and deepest of all, a parting from oneself.

The ascent to God is not a straight and continuous climb; it is a perpetual up and down. The aspiration to God succeeds only because our very falling away from him obliges us to put out all our energy again and again to recover from falls, setbacks, and slackening of effort. Our failure is in a sense necessary as a constant goad urging us on towards God. This explains the continually repeated lament of the believer that he is making no progress, that he has the impression he is still at the start of his journey to God. In this the Christian knows by shattering personal experience the sovereign liberty of the divine friendship: "I will have mercy on whom I have mercy, and I will have compassion on whom I have compassion. So it depends not upon man's will or exertion, but upon God's mercy" (Rom. 9, 15–16).

Nothing is given to man which by human right would be his anyway. Whatever God gives him is given out of mercy and pity. The mercy of God bestowed on man is adorable as the ground of our hope precisely because it is wholly and entirely God's absolutely free and sovereignly independent mercy. Everything in our life is submitted to the greatness of God's mercy, even (and above all) our sins. In the First Letter of John there is a sentence that gives us some idea of what it ultimately means for a broken and sinful human being to be wholly exposed to God's mercy: "By this we shall . . . reassure our hearts before him whenever our hearts condemn us; for God is greater than our hearts, and he knows everything" (1 Jn. 3, 19–20). God's power is thus made perfect in human weakness—the condition in which man is perpetually harassed by a messenger of Satan (cf. 2 Cor. 12, 6–10), so that he will humbly look up to that man who was given the promise, ". . . today you will be with me in Paradise" (Lk. 23, 43).

One of the key words of New Testament revelation is the word *kainos* in its various forms. It is a word that points to the goal of Christian promise. Christ everywhere speaks of something new, of a new beginning. He promises us a new heaven and a new earth, a new Jerusalem, the new wine of the eschatological banquet, a new name (a fundamentally transformed personality). According to Paul, the Christian is already a new man, the beginning of a new creation. At the same time, however, he is called upon to renew the inner man every day. The new man, and with him the new creation, the new Jerusalem, the new heaven, the new earth, the new name, the new song, the new cosmos, are already there; nevertheless, they have all still to be conquered in an interior struggle, a constantly new beginning. It is not at all surprising, therefore, that in the gospel the love of those who fail, of the sinners, the return of the prodigal son, is called blessed. These in fact give clearest expression to the situation that the Christian is in all the time—that of a radically new beginning. The tears of Magdalen and Peter, the humble prayer of the publican, the prayer of the repentant thief show the fundamental pattern of our holiness—total resignation of heart and destiny to God's mercy.

We may refer here to a theological insight that is often misunderstood but that, when rightly interpreted, is vitally important for us. According to a well-founded theological doctrine, the good works, merits, and previously achieved degree of virtues are restored, resuscitated in a person who turns to God again in contrition and amendment, even after a grave sin. This doctrine only needs to be freed from its abstract and partly grotesque, partly unintelligible terminology for us to rediscover something of the nature of the love of God and the mystery of human contrition. The good in one's life can never be lost, while the bad that happens in it through one's own fault is utterly eradicated (not merely forgotten but made non-existent). The liberation, courage, and joy that this can bring into our life can only be fully appreciated by the saints. How easily such ancient theses of theology, which are sometimes regarded with a certain condescending smile, can be translated into shatteringly vital truths. Might not this be an important task for the new theology?

We have spoken in some detail of the fundamental polarity of a life of holiness—the experience of the divine requirement and of human failure—in order to indicate the wider perspective in which the Christian has to wrestle with God to attain God. In what follows a few remarks will be enough, under each of twelve headings, to sketch the seemingly insoluble problems, paradoxes, apparent contradictions, antinomies, and clash of opposites in Christian holiness.

The Clash of Opposites

Fulfillment and Crucifixion

Christ comprised everything human in his own reality, once and for all. His human heart thus became the permanent center of all salvation. As Irenaeus of Lyons said in a theological statement that is still valid, the living man is the glory of God. In Christ, incomprehensible and unapproachable mystery become a human presence. Since then, the grace of God is as much a matter of course for us as our own life. It has become a gesture, a human encounter, a life, indistinguishable from ourselves and closely akin to all that is human, the fulfillment of our life, a sphere into which we can freely develop.

At the same time, however, we know that this selfsame grace makes us look fools in the eyes of the world, and not merely occasionally but permanently. We must never confuse the mercy and friendship of God towards us with our own instinct for life. The saints do not present us with examples of wonderful acts of renunciation "To be admired, but not imitated." The divine is a painful wound in our life; it says No to the purely human, to any all-too-human way of thinking about God. The quest for God makes us cry out, utter the cry of pain of the creature exposed to the divine, a cry that often re-echoes in the void and goes unheard. Grace always involves danger.

Perhaps in the domain of the Christian conception of man the contrary also holds good. God's presence is precisely what makes his remoteness most clearly felt. God's friendship makes man live in the unfathomable, incomprehensible, "burned out." But the sometimes suffocating loneliness of man in the presence of the Absolute is transformed into a blissfully direct awareness of God's presence, or even a "perception" of God. How this is possible, we cannot say; it is only possible to report that it is so. Explanations are lacking. We are simply trying here to formulate what is known to human beings who have inwardly experienced God and fully accepted his action within them—the knowledge and experience of the saints.

This experience was summed up on Christ's lips as a cry from one abandoned by God: "My God, my God, why hast thou forsaken me?" (Mk. 15, 34). The oldest account of the Passion, that of Mark (Matthew follows him in this), gives this cry to God in dereliction in Jesus' mother tongue, and as the only words spoken on the cross; these would therefore be Jesus' last words, and the original form of what he said on the cross. Luke, and then even more decidedly John, no longer bore the tension between presence and remoteness of God contained in Christ's last words, and attempted to replace them interpretatively by other sayings. But we should leave this saying as it is, ultimately impossible to interpret though it is, and await the moment when we ourselves can quite honestly repeat it after Jesus, in the realization that where God seems farthest away he is closest.

Promise and Defeat

Human life, if lived in a Christian way, belongs to the "last days." Christian life should be a symbol for the definitive transformation of the world. Two things have to be considered here.

110

The new, transfigured world, which has returned to God's realm, springs from the intrinsic ontological dynamism of the old world. The Greek Fathers, for example, liked to regard the universe as the cosmic mantel of the divinity. Consequently, God wants us to be devoted to the world, to its secular character as world. Even in the world we can already become aware of the forces of what is coming, of the impulsion towards the future. That is why the Christians have rightly been called the "soul of the world." In the *Letter to Diognetus*, the Christian is emphatically warned against flight from the world, "Such is the high post of duty in which God has placed them, and it is their moral duty not to shrink from it."

On the other hand, flight from the world can also be called a genuine and even radically Christian virtue. In this sense it consists of a total renunciation of all that is denoted by the biblical expressions "world" and "flesh." Now the "world" and the "flesh" denote everything belonging to the domain of what is visibly present and tangible. In other words, everything we can grasp and catch a glimpse of, even our innermost self, is still world and flesh, for it too belongs to the tangible realm and is in many ways beyond the reach of our intellectual powers, alienated. Our true reality is still hidden with Christ in God, the most inaccessible of all that is inaccessible, and will only be manifest when Christ our life visibly enters the world again (cf. Col. 3, 3–4). Our genuine being, and with it the transfigured universe, do not, after all, spring from within the old world but will come down from heaven as a sheer gift of God's love freely given, "prepared as a bride adorned for her husband" (Rev. 21, 2). The new will be something fundamentally different, not something that springs from the essence of this present world. In order to attain eternal stability, the world must perish. Expressed metaphorically, at

Christ's death the veil of the temple—the veil of the "world"—was rent from top to bottom (Mk. 15, 38; on the significance of this event cf. Heb. 10, 19–20). Once again holiness actually lived to the end consists in a "clash of opposites."

Action and Contemplation

The Ignatian formula *contemplativus in actione* ("contemplative in action," both contemplative and practical man) is easily repeated but hard to carry into effect. It combines two essentially different attitudes, for action is not contemplative recollection. Activity in the world always represents a threat to, or abandonment of, the interior life; it can even mean self-forgetfulness, "dissipation." Practical success is constantly bought at the cost of whittling down the absolute character of what is demanded. People's activity continually entangles them in themselves, hence the dullness of heart of the practical man. He becomes estranged from himself although, or rather because, he knows he is solidly established and recognized.

Contemplation, too, has many dangers. The contemplative is aware of the presumption of action. He puts his finger on what man is and pitilessly unmasks its fragility, hollowness, and pretense. But the contemplative himself is perhaps in even worse straits. Precisely at the point where he sinks into the ultimate meaningfulness, his own reality begins to disintegrate. His contemplation itself evaporates into the inexpressible. This experience is monstrous and deadly in effect. No human being can live without imagery and without language.

Perhaps the aparently desperate combination of these two opposed, equally dangerous attitudes is precisely the reason why the "Ignatian man" often gives such an impression of being disillusioned, skeptical, and sober (or even, sometimes, calculating). He is spiritually "demythologized," "disinfected," but for precisely that reason he is also a moderate. In his often burned-out heart, Christ can establish his rule, precisely because, for this kind of man, everything except God has become merely relative. But even God is thought of and treated in practice by him as *excessus*, as standing above all notions, measures, and dreams (*deus semper maior*).

Honor and Humility

What do these two ideas mean for the saint? In the continual collapse of his endeavors, his life builds up towards the eternal. In its flux he already lives in the domain of what endures. Human activity is a continual loss, but in that very fact he is aware of divine self-communication. Frustration, distraction, and unrest reduce his personal life to nothing, yet the love of God produces a constant interior deepening. His wealth amounts to very little, but this little makes him rich. His life is a perpetual death, a mortal fragility, a battlefield of the spirit, captivity and sterility. Nevertheless, by hope he already lives beyond death. Within, he is incorruptible. A peace that the world does not know radiates from him; he has the peace of the just in his soul. He already knows freedom; he is creative and joyous. He is a pilgrim who in a mysterious way has already arrived home, a stranger who already lives securely, resented yet welcome, a seeker who in fact has already found, and who can only really seek because he already lives in fulfillment. He is driven by longing, but eternal happiness has already entered his soul; he is full of hope, but already bears the object of his hope within him. His life is the life of everyday, but adorned in preparation for an eternal festival. His knowledge loses itself in mystery, yet his face is radiant with the presence of God. He is still walking in the night, but the dawn of a new day is already heralded.

What meaning does consciousness of personal worth, or humility, have for him? Simone Weil expressed the incomprehensible and indefinable character of Christian life, which transcends all the categories, in the following way. Someone who remains in the love of God may sink to the point where he can no longer hold back the cry: "My God, my God, why hast thou forsaken me?" If he perseveres there, however, without ceasing to love, he ultimately arrives at what is no longer either misfortune or joy (we might add, neither honor nor humility), but the pure, suprasensible quintessence of joy and sorrow (honor and humility), the love of God itself. John of the Cross could not make the point better.

Simplicity and Shrewdness

Simplicity, spiritual poverty, a limited outlook, innocence, and naïvety are combined in the biblical symbol of the dove. The saint accepts the gifts from God's hand without question, almost without thanks. When he uses them, his right hand does not know what his left hand is doing. He does not feel qualified to pass judgment on others or on himself. With simplicity he fulfills the will of him who gave him courage to dare to love. He does not see anything remarkable in the fact that the interior miracles of God's presence take place in him. He enters into God's friendship simply and unconcerned.

At the same time, however, he tests everything and exercises spiritual discernment. Everything on this earth is provisional for him, replaceable and ambiguous. He feels called upon to "plan"

114

grace, and "calculate" divine things. To do this he has to treat with reserve even the sublimest expression of the spirit (especially these). He regards all emotional enthusiasm with suspicion. His worst opponents are fanatics who want to make an absolute of what is finite and conditioned. "Be as wise as serpents"—he knows how to be careful, and skillfully avoids the attacks of his enemies. He answers the world's malice with well-considered prudence. His attitude towards life includes a certain element of mistrust and mild skepticism. Dove and serpent—the saint combines them not merely simultaneously in his own person, but in the single act of serving the transcendent in a world which is narrow and impenetrable and of which only the deceptive surface is visible. His true location lies far behind these confusing oppositions, at a point where his life is ecstatically absorbed in the divine abyss of love.

Necessity and Freedom

The souls of the saints were drawn irrevocably and irresistibly under the spell of the Absolute. The quieting of their human will effected an inner purification. Sometimes they were no longer even capable of arbitrary action. Nevertheless, they were free while persevering in the attitude of surrender, although it is true that they could not adopt any other. We catch sight here of the highest freedom which lies behind the apparent irresistible force and intrinsic necessity of love.

On occasion, everyday life itself shows us a reflection of this highest freedom, in the faces and actions of people who love one another. They are set free to accomplish the intrinsic necessity of what their beloved calls for from them. To be free ultimately means to be receptive to a gift that cannot be had by coercion, the ability to respond as partner to total devotion. Love is therefore the highest and authentic form of freedom. Precisely where freedom freely renounces itself, where in a supreme ecstasy of love it accepts its own extinction, the highest freedom is realized. The starting point from which a Christian metaphysics of freedom should be worked out is this basic experience of saints and lovers.

Immediate Presence and Obscurity

Every advance in knowledge of God brings greater simplicity into the idea of God. In the mystical experience of a direct relation with God, the representations of God are shattered. Words, images, and modes of expression merge and cancel one another out. Hegel in a different connection describes the same development in the *Phenomenology of Mind*: "Thought becomes formless, musical as it were, thought that no longer attains an objective concept." Thought about God becomes "recollection." In the mystical state, a man can no longer cling to anything. A great solitude grips the spirit. God himself, by withdrawing the mental representations of himself, seems to abandon everything of this world, including the soul. His approach to the saint brings nothingness with it. The nearer he comes, the less clear the lineaments of his face become, and the remoter he feels to human sensibility. Even "recollection" gradually disappears, in the sense that the human mind no longer thinks "of God," he thinks "God." In the end even this God becomes "nothing." Mystics did not even shrink from giving him this name: pure and naked nothingness, absolutely transcending all designations and positive determinations. What they were able to say about God over and above this were "statements" of their inexpressible waiting for the uncircumscribed and ineffable. But this waiting, this ultimate depth of human hope, shows what an "all" this "nothing" was for them.

Experience and Practice

The saint's thinking becomes increasingly simple. His feelings and acts of will are extinguished. His whole personal life becomes bottomless, unfathomable, concentrates into a single point where all acts are posited even before they are performed, where everything is virtually one and remains undifferentiated. Man is there identical with the non-conceptual, transcendental dynamism of his being. Sometimes the mystics call this ultimate essentiality the "apex of the soul," sometimes the "center" or "ground" of the soul. Man no longer waits for God by means of loving thoughts, feelings, and acts of the will. The relation to God flows from the wellspring of the whole personality in a way that is incomprehensible to the mystic himself. The prayer of the saint is reduced to one heartfelt, scarcely perceptible word, a Yes of consent, in which the whole expectation of the creation is concentrated, and man becomes the summit and spearhead of the cosmos.

Vitality and Passivity

With this Yes, complete silence has fallen on the soul of the saint. He still of course sums up his life in hope, but even this happens more and more rarely and only as the expression of a predominant passivity. Francis de Sales uses the simile of the statue. The contemplative life is like a statue that fulfills the will of its creator simply by remaining in the attitude which he has determined for it. The different acts of faith, love, thankfulness, trust, and so forth, gradually merge into a general attitude of dependence on God. Piety is reduced more and more to a simple glance. Loving attention to the presence of God and his guidance permeates the whole daily round and becomes the essential act of contemplation. This remarkable "practice," which fundamentally is not one, but merely self-abandonment to God's will, comprises the whole of life. Marie de l'Incarnation lived for years with a constant consciousness of the presence of God, and despite her work in a big firm was continually absorbed in prayer. It is as if the human being were waiting, overcome by a kind of paralysis, for the inexpressible. This "supernatural suspension" of the powers of the soul is man's total incapacity in face of the incomprehensibility of the Absolute. It was something of the sort that affected Thomas Aquinas when, months before his physical collapse, God took the pen from his hand and made him realize that all he had written was "straw." Before ultimate departure the soul falls silent.

Prayer and Prayerlessness

The outer structure of the life of prayer gradually crumbles. Usually the prayer of petition goes first and simply merges into the flow of contemplation. John of the Cross says that if a man who lives deep in prayer in the state of contemplative union with God is asked by a friend to pray for him, he will probably soon forget the request, his memory is so deeply absorbed in God, unless God himself, with the intention of answering the petition, reminds him of it at the proper moment.

But something even more fundamental takes place. The contemplative becomes indifferent to all that he could ask for from

God, because he knows that he himself and his friends, the whole world in fact, are secure within the all-embracing loving kindness of God. Francis de Sales said that the soul should renounce its eternal happiness and willingly accept damnation if it knew that this were God's will. We find the same attitude in Catherine of Siena and Angela of Foligno. The idea is not even far from the sober Ignatius of Loyola. It would be too easy to dismiss all this as a hypothesis *per impossibile*, an opinion based on an impossible supposition. They are really expressions of pure love.

The mystic enters a state of remoteness from God in which his consciously formulated (categorial) prayer disappears, and he appears to be abandoned to peridition. The soul is overwhelmingly conscious of its unworthiness of God, just as every lover feels unworthy of his beloved. Nevertheless, the saint persists in waiting for God, in silence, without formulated prayer, hoping against hope. A possible explanation of this tragic character of holiness is probably to be found in the fact that the despairing condition referred to only affects the outer powers of the soul (in reality, all of ourselves that is usually known to us); it is not able to penetrate into the actual ground of the soul, which is where loving contact with God is experienced. Prayer therefore plunges man into an abyss of remoteness from God, where he cannot "pray," where he even experiences reprobation, so that he may be definitively re-created on that basis of uttermost helplessness.

Self-Development and Loss of Self

The contemplative senses God within him and fixes his gaze upon him. He penetrates more and more deeply into his own self until he comes so close to himself that he loses sight of himself. Contemplation of God leads the mystic to union with God. God alone now appears to stand in the place of the self. Explicitly to reflect on these mysterious events in his own soul would banish God from this central position. Not even gratitude would induce a mystic to do that. Any reflection, in fact, would be a betrayal. It would mean breaking the bow of contemplation and snapping the bond of union merely for the sake of turning one's attention to oneself again. What is quite natural to us, and indeed an intellectual necessity, namely, that of reflecting on the experiences we have lived through, becomes for the mystic a temptation to abandon God and mirror himself. The slightest turning back on himself could bring down the interior castle of contemplation, and put an end to what is essentially ec-static. These ecstatics live in very great danger. Their vocation is to accomplish the eternal glory of union with God even now in their fragile personal life, and endure this happiness amid earthly inauthenticity.

Contemplation and Virtue

The contemplative does not lose virtue, but he loses his former attitude towards it. To be inseparably united to God within him is all he can aim at. He cannot endure any longer anything possessed or practiced. He perseveres in a perpetually renewed waiting for God. Consequently, he cannot have anything to do with habits, however noble and sacred. His own situation lies beyond the virtues, at their source.

Furthermore, he suffers from continual temptations. He feels as if his whole being were a prey to temptation and disorder. How simple and humanly satisfying it would be to counter these temptations with the practice of the virtues, if only he could do so! But the outer powers of the soul are suspended (by God himself), so that he may wait upon God in the center of his soul. Consequently, he does not feel that he is "virtuous" at all. To the outside observer, his confessor for example, he indeed seems a model of heroic virtue. In his own eyes, however, he feels as if he were entirely a prey to sin, and even to damnation. The only appropriate phrase to describe this state of supreme desolation is Luther's *simul justus et peccator* ("both just and sinner"). On his deathbed, John of the Cross answered one of his brethren who was trying to encourage him by pointing out the good works he had done, "Don't say that, Father, don't say that! Tell me my sins!"

Such is the distress of the just on earth. Anyone who regards himself as just is a sinner, while anyone who honestly confesses himself in his heart of hearts to be a sinner, is just. As Christ said, "This man went down to his house justified rather than the other" (Lk. 18, 14). The existence of the saint, as actually lived, is a tension between beatitude and damnation.

We have tried by means of the experiences of the saints and mystics to mark out the domain of personal life where the Absolute is awaited in hope, and to define its tensions. It is our good fortune and that of theology, that the Church has accepted the risk of setting up human beings with experiences of this kind as models, and even encourages us to emulate them. Living experience of the Absolute threatens to strike at the very root of much that has been systematically elaborated. Objectification, depersonalization, and institutionalization, all the fascination of the tangible, is radically called in question. Sometimes that has led to a difference of standpoint between the official Church and its saints in matters regarding salvation. But the inner protest of the *ecclesia spiritualis* is an integral part of the Church itself. Anyone who deliberately tips the balance in favor of the institutional to the detriment of the spiritual should clearly realize what a victory of the institutional would have meant for the Church and even for the world. The saints succeeded time and time again in preventing it. Perhaps the spiritual content of Christian hope, of departure far into the radically unknown, would have been sacrificed to every imaginable kind of secular interest, and to a large extent the Church would have ceased to be transparent to the transcendent. It is high time we reflected more than ever on the often confusing experiences of the saints and believers and shaped our theology accordingly, a theology of living hope as actually experienced.

In all our considerations, one fundamental insight constantly recurs in different applications: self-realization is achieved by self-sacrifice. A theology of vitally experienced hope, such as we have just postulated, would have to develop this insight as basis, as a sort of fundamental theology of hope. That is what we wish to attempt to do in the next meditation. If it is true in practice that we only really possess what we give away, it must also be true that we only possess hope by giving hope to others. What that means and where such an attitude can lead can only be discussed if what is in the depth of the human heart, mercy, is allowed to speak. We know God so little. We have formed innumerable ideas of God and thought out innumerable names for him. Sometimes we are afraid that he is none of these. But we know our brethren better. It is easier for us to speak about them. If we do so, perhaps we shall catch a better glimpse of our incarnate God than by means of concepts and ideas. Our brethren are God's messengers in the mysterious sense that they bear the author of the message within them, and, what is more, are that author himself.

6

Everyday Hope

From the beginning, the community of the Christian Church knew fear and anxiety. Christ indeed revealed himself to the disciples in the fullness of his power. They understood that Jesus of Nazareth is Lord of all, the Kyrios before whose power every knee in heaven and on earth and under the earth should bend (cf. Phil. 2, 9–11). But this realization was precisely what paralyzed them. Christ's disciples already foresaw that a state of authentic but transcendent life lay ahead of them. At the start, their powers, and perhaps their nerves, failed them in face of this overwhelming revelation. They even hid themselves, torn between anxiety and confidence, "in the supper room, where they were staying . . . with one accord devoted themselves to prayer . . ." (Acts 1, 13–14).

This situation can be detached from its historical conditions and regarded as exemplifying a fundamental feature of Christian life. We too feel empty, disappointed, and broken. Yet in this state of depression, we, like the disciples at that time, have to keep up our brethren's hope. What Christ's friends felt can and must be incorporated into Christian spirituality. For in our life and even in that of Christ's Church, there can be times of particular weariness when God makes special demands on us, although we are timid, broken, and without initiative, so that we have to be, and can be, signs of hope for others. These are the times when the Christian hears the call to bear witness referred to by St. Paul: "What is our hope . . .? Is it not you?" (1 Thess. 2, 19).

How does a fainthearted life turn into powerful hope for one's fellow men? The answer is both modest and lofty: by the works of mercy. They are God's promises carried into effect in daily life for the brothers and sisters of Christ. Our mercy has not only to lessen and lighten humanity's physical and mental help-lessness; it has also to build a bridge between heaven and earth, between anxiety and confidence. The Church has given the name "corporal and spiritual works of mercy" to the things that the bewildered appeal to us for to give hope to them and to others. In that way it has exactly described what hope has to be from day to day.

Feed the Hungry

Christ radically equated that fundamental impulse of the human heart which we call love of our fellow man with the love of God. The two together sum up the old covenant. In Christ's picture of the day of judgment, love of neighbor is actually the only criterion for admission to the kingdom of God. In other words that is what decides our eternal lot and what concerns the inner-most constitution of the order of salvation. What brings us salva-tion, heaven, to us? The simple, often unnoticed works of active charity. Everything else, however fine and important, including even knowledge of God and faith, is only a part. Even the criterion of martyrdom pales in comparison with love of the neighbor, and therefore does not represent the really serious business of the Christian's life: ". . . if I deliver my body to be burned, but have not love, I gain nothing" (1 Cor. 13, 3). The love referred to here simply means, in the first place, feeding the hungry.

This makes real bodily hunger as we know it in its terrible reality at the present time the object of the kind of love of neighbor that brings salvation. In addition an interior attitude is meant, quite simply that of self-sacrifice. Not just what we do and the gifts we bring, but we ourselves, what we are, should be food for others. In this connection we really need to rethink Christ's eucharistic attitude. In his mysterious anticipation of his death—perhaps already in the certainty of it—Christ became totally himself. He had, of course, always been so, but never with this utter intensity. And so his person became totally present for others. For in human life, self-realization and self-sacrifice always go together; they mutually condition and complement each other. Accordingly, wherever a presence of this kind occurs, even if it is a purely human one, there is found a figure of the Eucharist, a feeding of human beings with the nourishment of one's own being. Generous self-giving in this not exclusive but complementary sense would be "eucharistic."

This supplementary view of the eucharistic attitude allows us to understand the sacrament of encounter with Christ, the epitome of our faith (*mysterium fidei*), in a sense that extends beyond holy Mass and even beyond the circle of Catholics and Christians. Every human being, as Karl Rahner has frequently emphasized, whether Christian or pagan, indifferent to God in everyday life or atheist, who rebels against names, ideas, customs, and institutions but not against the incomprehensible mystery of God, has already a share in the Eucharist, by giving his personal attention and presence to a fellow human being in need, and so reproduces Christ's attitude towards life. How exactly a man is to fulfill this exacting demand and realize it in his own life in a different way in each particular instance can only be discovered by the individual himself. That is precisely what will make him a full member of the Church, even if he knows nothing about the Church. In other words, it will make him a human being who contributes something irreplaceable to the eucharist of life, irreplaceable because only he can do it, completing in his own life what Christ could no longer do. As Paul writes, ". . . in my flesh [in my earthly life] I complete what is lacking in Christ's afflictions for the sake of his body, that is, the Church" (Col. 1, 24).

Give Drink to the Thirsty

When Christ promised his friends the inner principle of a transcendent testimony—the "Spirit" and the "Comforter"—he also added something strange, which at first sight does not seem to have anything to do with consolation at all: "And when he [the Comforter] comes he will convince the world of sin . . ." (Jn. 16, 8). The spirit of God is to bring to light the sin of the world. Despite appearances to the contrary, this means an inner liberation. Things are clear at last; one knows just how one stands. It is possible to be completely honest. In our life there is sin, not just the sort of half-light described by words like delusion, weakness, and guilt, but something that one can confess with contrition before God. It is the Holy Spirit's doing when man begins to speak of his sin in a repentant spirit, when a frail being no longer wanders about in the wilderness of his own offenses, almost dying of thirst, but returns to the wellspring of forgiveness.

Who are the thirsty in the world around us? Their voices are scarcely audible, they are so faint, or so confused. What can a human being say to us, when he feels nothing but the dryness of his own failure, the poverty of his own heart? A human being stands in front of us who cannot even make his voice heard in the searing flame of his own guilt. Now Christ promised the helpful Christian—every Christian, not only the priest—"a spring of water welling up" in him, that is, the water of mercy, forgiveness, and grace. Christ himself, on the cross, in the desert of human dereliction, uttered man's hoarse cry: "I thirst" (Jn. 19, 28).

To give drink to the thirsty, therefore, means to listen even for the voice of those who are no longer able to express their distress. This may help a threatened person suddenly to realize that someone else is with him, sinful and tormented by doubt, tormented with thirst himself, but mercifully bringing him, all the same, relief for his thirst. Perhaps this man has no solution, no answer to give, but at least his presence does good, refreshes, brings relief. By saying, "You are not alone" in the desolate aridity and exhaustion of life, and faithfully repeating it, he creates new hope. This is no facile consolation he brings by acquiescing in the other's revolt. He does not agree, if he may not; he does not permit, as far as in him lies, anything to be done that would not be right. His gift is clear, crystal clear. And suddenly the springs begin to flow, new abundance wells up in the other's soul, life where before there was mere drought and meaninglessness. The sufferer is out in the open again. He has finally found shelter with a human being and therefore a gleam of hope.

Clothe the Naked

Life is "naked" when it is exposed, cold, and in danger—three claims on our mercy.

The worst human indignity consists in exposure. A private matter, the most precious thing the person has in his life or some cruel secret that he would like to hide in shame, is dragged out into the light of public knowledge and gossip. The stricken victim is numb, feels lost, robbed. Other people's gossip forces him to disguise himself, and a life of alienation from self ensues. Anyone who identifies himself with his life as other people talk about it risks falling into an utter loss of self-respect and confidence. Compassion should make us realize, however, that the innermost events in the soul are so mysteriously interwoven, and are marked by so many experiences, motives, fears, and joys, that quite often a person does not know himself what is happening inside him. But if someone comes along who is kind and experienced, sympathetic but respectfully reserved and silent, humiliation is covered up, clothed in good will. A man can once again be what he is within himself. To understand people sympathetically, not to force them into acting a part, and consequently into self-estrangement, to respect their mystery, not to tolerate their exposure, is another way of saying "to clothe the naked." In our presence, no one should be subjected to exposure.

Nakedness means deadly cold. The Church sees one of the effects of the Holy Spirit as restoring warmth to something that has gone cold within us. Someone who meets with too much rejection and coldness from those around begins to be penetrated by it through and through, which makes him icy and hard, destroying what is warm and vital in him. If we are to bring hope to a chilled and apathetic life of this kind, we must carefully and gradually give small signs of kindness (gradually, because sudden contact with warmth can cause burns in a frozen body, and even more in an icy soul), until the blood begins to circulate and the soul comes to life again. Christ's demand here is that in our presence no one should perish of cold.

Edzard Schaper once pointed out the old saying that someone escaped from some misfortune "with his bare life." All any of us really have is our "bare life." Not much is left, only a small remnant salvaged from our whole life until now. Not much more is likely to be added to it. Fine and important experiences, perhaps, but probably nothing essential. Job lamented, "Naked I came from my mother's womb, and naked shall I return" (Job 1, 21). One day this life in its utter nakedness and poverty will be "clothed" in God's mercy. "This perishable nature must put on the imperishable, and this mortal nature must put on immortality" (1 Cor. 15, 53). "To clothe the naked" also means, therefore, to make our provisional world transparent to heaven, by cultivating the thought of the resurrection and of heaven.

There is much more that might be said on this topic, for example, what Christ understood by "clothing" and how a person was healed by touching the hem of his garment. Meditative reflection will recognize essential truths in that connection (cf. Mt. 9, 20; Mt. 17, 2; Jn. 19, 23; Rev. 1, 13; Mt. 22, 11; Lk. 15, 22; Rev. 7, 9–14). What we have tried to point out is simply that Christ was not thinking so much of organizations and official services, although they do much good, and often much more Christian good than we do, but of something radically personal, not so much a program as an experience of the presence of God in a world still not transparent to him.

Show Hospitality to Strangers

How transitory man is is brought home to us nowadays by the
actual presence of strangers, foreigners, and aliens, whose distress
is only too painfully evident. Man is *homo viator*: he is constantly
moving, traveling perpetually, always en route. He can be regarded, from one point of view or another, as having lost his
way, a tramp, a wanderer, or a pilgrim. And the travel metaphor
does not mean that he is making straight for a particular goal
or destination; on the contrary, it often reflects his vain attempts
to set his mind on any destination at all.

Some present-day philosophical interpretations of authentic
human existence have taken up again the Christian idea of man's
pilgrimage. Ernst Bloch notes that the essential in man is always
outstanding, waiting; Heidegger, that the ways we follow are
always woodland paths that suddenly peter out in trackless forest.
Not only is our life made up of expectation, but even more
radically it is an expectation of expectations which themselves
are waiting for further expectations, as Sartre puts it. For Marcel,
hope is the very stuff of which our soul is made. All these are
simple variations on the theme expressed by Pascal's description
of human existence: *"Ainsi nous ne vivons jamais, mais nous
espérons de vivre"* (*Pensées*, 172).

To be acutely conscious of this is perhaps the greatest grace
given to our age, but sets what is probably the most important
problem facing Christian piety today. How are we, by what are
we, to offer shelter, welcome, and a little peace to strayed, lost,
lonely human beings?

To realize the full harshness of what this demands, we must

130

take the word "alien" very seriously, with the full force that the English, for example, give instinctively to the word "foreigner." The alien stranger is really foreign to us, that is, his customs, attitude towards life, ways of thought, and style of life are quite different from ours. His attitude towards us and his motives are unknown or difficult to fathom. His reactions are sometimes incalculable. Even his God is unfamiliar. So we mistrust him, and would not bring him into our house. We only offer him a home because Christ has identified himself with him. By doing so we become aware of our own vulnerability. The alien is merely the embodiment of our own condition, our inner home-lessness, our insecurity, anxiety, our alienation from ourselves and from one another. Longing for an ultimate home grows from offering the hospitality of a home. We should be grateful to the alien. He has enriched us, not we him.

Deliver Captives, Set Prisoners Free

A brief note only on this point. Christ told us clearly and un-mistakably that in any prisoner we visit, we visit Christ himself. There have been times in the history of the Church—sociologi-cally conditioned, no doubt, but they reveal the depth of the Christian attitude—when Christians sold themselves in order to ransom others from slavery. Even physical captivity can be an expression of supreme inner freedom. Christ himself gave his own limited and unsuccessful life, typified by his imprisonment before his death on the cross, an ultimate meaning of inner liberation by accepting it. What took place once and for all in the life of Christ has to be realized daily in our own life: freedom in captivity.

We are all prisoners, each in a different way. Life itself is still fettered in us. Our pains, obligations, the responsibilities we have voluntarily undertaken are only a small part of what we might have been. The inclinations that have gradually taken shape in us, our friendships and our love, all limit our horizon, for they only partly fulfill us. Our affections cling to what we have and what is possible, but that holds us back from other, perhaps even more wonderful, possibilities. Worry, humiliation, and frustration chain us to the drab cruelty of the daily round. Our own body is often a prison cell to us. We only notice this when it begins to threaten us and cramp our minds. And, deepest of all, we are imprisoned by the strange and sinister thing we call sin, something essentially alien to us yet often inescapably close.

A description of the essential features of human captivity, a study of the symptoms of imprisonment in the human condition, is found in Dante's *Purgatorio*. External visions reveal an interior landscape of man's soul, the place where man is captive. Man looks upwards and waits in silence for deliverance. "I saw that goodly host stand sentinel,/Thereafter, speechless, in expectant love/Scanning the sky with lowly looks, all pale" (*Purg.,* VIII, 22–24). Man has to climb seven terraces to reach final liberation. Each stage represents a stage of existential purification. The transition from one terrace to another costs effort, but the higher one climbs, the easier the ascent becomes, not because the path is easier but because the human being is less burdened. The transformation takes place in this way. First, pride is atoned for and humility achieved, then envy is overcome and magnanimity attained. Hardness of heart is changed to meekness. Sloth gives way to joy in action; covetousness is stripped away and liberality takes its place. Excess is broken and self-control learned. Lust is burned pure in repentance. To set captives free, therefore, in another sense means showing others by living example that it is possible to satisfy our longing for deliverance even now in our earthly captivity. It means proving that it is possible even on earth to live in the attitude that is a condition for entry into the Paradiso. "No word from me, no further sign expect; /Free, upright, whole, thy will henceforth lays down/Guidance that it were error to neglect,/Whence o'er thyself I mitre thee and crown" (*Purg.*, XXVII, 139–141). By living our hope we should be an "angel" (God's messenger) for our brother, breaking open the carefully bolted cell of his own self, as an angel once did the door of Peter's dungeon (cf. Acts 12, 8–17).

Visit the Sick

To be sick also means "waiting for someone," despite pain, confusion, and depression—like the sick man by the mysterious pool in Jerusalem, who lay there for decades and waited patiently until in the end someone came by and took pity on him (Jn. 5, 1–16). That wait lasted thirty-eight years. Year after year the sick man saw how the water was troubled and healed others. He tried so often to drag himself down to it by his own powers. He had already begged so many other men to help him. Then, unexpectedly, the great day came that he had ceased even to hope for. He was able to tell a human being his greatest grief, even greater than the pain of his illness: "I have no one." There was no reproach or bitterness in what he said, only regret and helplessness.

Perhaps we shall not be able to cure illness or even relieve pain by our visit. We can do one thing at least: show the sick, most probably without saying so, merely by our presence, that they are a grace for us, that the world would be unthinkable and unendurable without the support of those who suffer. Christ went down into the depths of human distress. Consequently, the transformation of the world into Christ's divine and human reality takes place in suffering—precisely there, in fact. It is probably one of the greatest graces of visiting the sick that we can bear witness before the world to Christ's positive, encouraging, hopeful attitude expressed in the words of the Second Letter to the Corinthians: "I seek not what is yours but you" (2 Cor. 12, 14).

Bury the Dead

A feature of human life is a kind of friendship with the dead, with people who have gone from us; it is a deep, silent, numbing pain. Christ felt it at the death of his friend Lazarus. But that death had a mysteriously deep effect in the life of Christ. A whole new aspect of death, full of unexpected hope, was opened up—death as "glorification of the son of God" (Jn. 11, 4). The death of someone we love can become a gift and a grace for us despite the pain that fills the foreground. That person is, of course, already safe in God's mercy. But we have "buried" the memory of him into our life. As Rilke said: "As regards myself, what died, died into my own heart." In other words, we think of the good and fine things the dead person did in his life, and of the possibilities that are still open to him, thus repeatedly rendering him present in our life, drawing on the beauty of a life that is already united with God. We are completing his earthly life for him and sharing in a destiny united to God. Perhaps people will one day think of us in this way.

In the essay "After Ten Years," which Dietrich Bonhoeffer

composed for fellow conspirators at Christmas 1942, he writes: "We are not Christs, but if we want to be Christians, we must know something of Christ's breadth of sympathy by acting responsibly, by grasping our 'hour,' by facing danger like free men, by displaying a real sympathy that springs, not from fear, but from the liberating and redeeming love of Christ for all who suffer. To look on without lifting a helping hand is most un-Christian. The Christian does not have to wait until he suffers himself; the sufferings of his brethren for whom Christ died are enough to awaken his active sympathy" (p. 24). Christians should begin their examination of conscience at these concrete points of "the sufferings of his brethren." Am I still serviceable as a witness to hope? This is what Bonhoeffer does at the end of the essay just quoted. "We have been the silent witnesses of evil deeds. Many storms have gone over our heads. We have learned the art of deception and of equivocal speech. Experience has made us suspicious of others, and prevented us from being open and frank. Bitter conflicts have made us weary and even cynical. Are we still serviceable?"

If we are to form a sober judgment of where we stand, what we have done to promote hope, the future possibilities we have to risk, the deeper dangers of the route we have to take, it has to be done in the light of Christ's unconditional claim on our hope. This involves what are called the spiritual works of mercy. These will be considered in the next meditation.

7

The Spirit of Hope

Those who have known what it is to be freed from great mental distress and brought out again into light and joy by God lose all desire to pass judgment and bear grudges. They feel the same if God has sent them someone to whom they can open their minds. They knew that helpless people are apt to resent the offer of help, don't want assistance. Nevertheless, they came to realize that the helping hand to freedom was fraternally given in God's name. All they want now is to help share their neighbor's troubles, to serve, help, forgive unconditionally and endlessly. It is experiences of this kind that encourages spiritual growth in those who are enabled to open out new horizons of forgiveness and hope for others, to understand their mental distress and help them bear it. Spiritual men of this kind, sealed with the Spirit, have existed in Christianity from the beginning. They are an integral part of the Church. In a certain sense, each of us is a man of the spirit, for each of us sooner or later is called to alleviate the mental suffering of his brethren by the spiritual works of mercy, and thereby find relief for his own mind and spirit.

What is the structure of the suffering that is endemic to the human spirit?

Correct Sinners

It is a particularly onerous undertaking to tell a fellow man: "If you go on in the way you are doing you will ruin your life." It serves to foster hope, nevertheless. To explain this, we have to look a little deeper.

The great confusion of the world in general and of our age in particular consists in the fact that man can no longer combine two things that stand together in a verse of Psalm 51: the prayer for a clean heart and the desire for a new spirit. Yet, as Gerhard Ebeling says, if Christians owe the world anything at the present time, it is, as it has always been, not primarily morality, philosophy, or politics, but faith, which purifies the heart. The new and world-transforming spirit follows almost of itself from a pure heart. The expression "create" ("Create in me a clean heart, O God, and put a new and steadfast spirit within me," Ps. 51, 10), is used in Hebrew only for God's action. God is therefore acting directly through anyone who brings his brother to a change of heart. God himself, through him, establishes a new beginning and opens a new page in history.

What is fundamentally at stake? Why do people feel so driven to beg God for a clean heart? In the first place, it is simply a question of being true, honest, that is, plain and straightforward with oneself. But this happens only if man submits himself to God's judgment (to the scrutiny of his love) and prays "God, be merciful to me a sinner." Contrition is not the virtue of the weak but of the inwardly strong. If a human being rids his soul of poison by contrition, he can face a new future cheerfully.

It was precisely the saints, people of unimpaired inner vitality, radiating the power of goodness and purity into the dark places of the world, who spent their whole lives in contrition and penance. Contrition shows that a soul is still sensitive to what is new, different, and better, still fresh, still able to withdraw from the evil lurking in the heart, and capable of making a radically new beginning. It is therefore an essential condition of the possibility of genuine joy, and of a new light-heartedness in face of reality. It is a youthfulness of the soul, the heart's capacity for transformation. The poorest of the poor are those who can no longer manage to feel remorse. A person in that state has no real future, no "new spirit."

If we are to define the fundamental situation regarding fraternal correction, and describe just what it involves, we must first notice that what happens in it is that a new spirit is awakened in a repentant heart. This is not something that should create disparity and provoke divisions among Christians. After all, they all have to feel that they are sinners. There is no difference between them in that respect. Of course, there is a difference in the insight and honesty with which people take responsibility for their sins before God. The real difference can be seen in the example of the two thieves who were crucified with Christ. Both were sinners, both revolted against the man who was dying with them, and derided him. Then, however, a mysterious change took place through the power of pain, which made one of them rebuke the other who had been reviling with him, and to beg Christ to remember him in his kingdom. The inner transformation is summed up in the words, "We indeed justly" (Lk. 23, 41). By this confession, the thief escaped from the frustration of his own guilt and the hopeless futility of his sufferings. Not so the other. Both were placed in the same situation; both had to die by crucifixion. Their external situation did not change in any way. Nevertheless, one became inwardly free, but the other remained closed.

This remarkable event (which, of course, is not intended to say anything about the eternal salvation of the so-called "unrepentant thief") is closely bound up with Christ's redemptive death, and shows quite clearly that the right of fraternal correction only belongs to those who acknowledge and confess their own sinfulness. That alone gives them power and authority to reprove others and only then in language that begins with an honest "We." The same event also indicates that in a Christian perspective there is no situation of irrevocable entanglement that cannot be intrinsically transformed by a humble confession of sin, or cannot take on a new and higher meaning from the words "We indeed justly." There is no place of terror that cannot become a sanctuary, a scene in the history of salvation, the return of a lost world. Even the worst wickedness has at least this much meaning, that it can bring realization of the inner misery of wickedness and transform it into praise. For a Christian, no one is irrevocably lost.

This attitude must be the basis of the charism of fraternal exhortation (Rom. 12, 8). The admonition takes place in an atmosphere of encouragement, edification, brotherliness, peacefulness, and gentleness (see Gal. 6, 1–5; 1 Thess. 5, 11. 15; 2 Thess. 3, 14–15; 2 Tim. 2, 25–26). The person who admonishes "saves" and "brings back" the sinner (Jas. 5, 19–20). He is not to heed his brother's status, but only his need (cf. Gal. 2, 14: "But when I [Paul] saw that they were not straightforward about the truth of the gospel, I said to Cephas before them all . . ."). It is often very difficult to discover how this kind of fraternal help can be given—where and when, for example, something decisive and clear can be said, where even an attitude of rejection (cf. Mt. 18, 15–17; Tit. 3, 10; 2 Thess. 3, 14; Jude 22–23) may effect a conversion, and when one must go down oneself into the same danger as the brother in order to "bring him back" (cf. Jas. 5, 19–20).

It is not given to all of us to share fully in other people's burdens and temptations and to feel for their inner disorder. It would be fatal for some to try to do so. That is why Paul gives the good advice: "Brethren, if a man is overtaken in any trespass, you who are spiritual should restore him in a spirit of gentleness. Look to yourself, lest you too be tempted" (Gal. 6, 1). It is impossible to lay down any generally valid rule of behavior here. Each one must find out for himself before God when, how, and whom he can "bring back," where he can open out a new future of hope for his brethren. We can only point out the duty and the spirit of fraternal correction.

The Christian's attitude in the matter will be determined by the way Paul spoke to the Philippians: "So if there is any encouragement in Christ, any incentive of love, any participation in the Spirit, any affection and sympathy, complete my joy by being of the same mind, having the same love, being in full accord and of one mind" (Phil. 2, 1–2).

Instruct the Ignorant

Martin Buber called the perplexing mystery of our time the "eclipse of God," and made it the title of one of his books. This darkness cannot be mastered, less now in fact than it ever could, by learned debates, the use of theological jargon and abstractions. For what is happening at present can only be described, to put it plainly, as "the experiment of eliminating God." For many people nowadays, just as for Christ's disciples long ago, our God has become a God who has been killed.

One of the most torturing experiences at the present time is that often when we speak about God we are merely dealing with dead formulas, empty concepts, big words, checks drawn with nothing in the bank. This lifeless talk about God does not for the most part flow from belief. One of the reasons many believing Christians find it so tedious dealing with atheists is that they will insist on talking endlessly about God. That kind of talk about God can and should die away, precisely because it does not come from the heart; people merely have the word "God" on their lips. The ancient maxim of theological studies, that inner conviction is what makes the real theologian, is still as valid as ever. The Christian will never convince anyone by intellectual acrobatics; in fact, strictly speaking, he will never really "win" anyone for God. What he does is, out of love for God, to bear witness to the mystery of God's love. It is a hopeful sign that the younger generation of Christians has declared nonexistent the God who has been talked to death, talked out of existence.

The same thing applies to the anonymous God. What you set your heart on, said Luther in his Exposition of the First Commandment, is, fundamentally speaking, your God. For faith, it is never a case of "God in himself," but only of "God experienced," the "God of my life." He stands outside formulas, concepts, and systems. He is what is innermost, most hidden, and most essential in the destiny of the individual human being. And so in Christian life, an ever purer and greater idea of God should in time crystallize out in a gradual process of personal encounter, out of small, fragmentary experiences of God, all of

141

them exposed to error and confusion. Wherever the God of our life becomes an intense presence, an awareness of vocation, a man knows that his life has a direction and a goal. He knows that he is not thrown out of nothing into nothing. Whatever the detours, false turns, and wrong roads he takes, he knows where he really comes from, where fundamentally he stands, where ultimately he is going, and what the inner mystery of his life is. A new path is always being opened out for him, so that he has enough light at least for his next step. The God who is defined but not directly addressed, who has become anonymous, is not "God for men." The God of our life does not make it impossible for us to speak; he is not inexpressible or nameless. If all names fail, there is still the one our love has given him, and continues to give him in innumerable ways: "You."

The God who has been killed is also a remote God. In the Bible, this distant God is called "the God of the godless": "They say to God, 'Depart from us!'" (Job 21, 14). If mention is made in the Bible of God's "terror," it is only because God humbles the proud and destroys self-righteousness. It is noteworthy that in Psalm 10, for example, "proud" is used as the contrary to "poor" and so determines the meaning of the latter term. The proud are those who afflict and oppress the souls of others; God is far from them. On the other hand, "O Lord thou wilt hear the desire of the meek; thou wilt strengthen their heart, thou wilt incline thine ear . . ." (Ps. 10, 17). But the transgressors will be put to shame by the "God of the poor." For the human being who has recognized and acknowledged his inner poverty, God could not be closer than he is. For him, God is the very picture of fulfillment composed by all his desires and aspirations. Such an idea of God is legitimate as long as human unfulfillment exists and there is anyone brave enough to admit his own fragility and need.

There is a further point that has to be taken into consideration here. To the poor in spirit, God is most evident, as a matter of course. Only a person who "does the truth" (Jn. 3, 21) and "does his will" (Jn. 7, 17) feels God's closeness and can know him. It is inherent in the mystery that God is that he only bestows his presence on those who have entered into the very essence of his revelation by the fact that their own actions convey revelation to their fellow men. Even the enunciation of divine truth, the instruction of the ignorant, cannot dispense with this essential factor in knowledge of God. The God who is close to us, the God of our life, the living You of our aspirations, cannot become an object of abstract proofs, but only the You to whom testimony is borne. Where the living God is really in question, mere talk that commits one to nothing must cease. Even rigorous deductive thought must turn into invocation.

Counsel the Doubtful

This precept is not to be regarded as a condemnation of doubt. Doubt is not God's adversary. As God-seekers, we all live lives of uncertainty and risk. This lack of clarity which is inherent in the exercise of faith in those seeking God ("Lord, I believe; help my unbelief") may appear to be darkness or even abandonment by God. But to regard it as a threat to faith itself would be a fundamental misunderstanding of our actual concrete situation in regard to faith. God's request to us to give good counsel to those in doubt, by a generous and understanding attitude, means rather that we are to try to prevent our brother's doubt from turning into despair. Two points are to be noted here.

As regards the first, we must realize that the bare will is sufficient. Words may break down on occasion, and the most assured landmarks that orientate us may fail us, mystery may become overwhelming, and the feeling of our own powerlessness utterly crush us. But that merely proves that none of those things are decisive. Where salvation occurs is where man raises empty hands to God, perhaps not even in a gesture of petition but in one of uncomprehending, unknowing devotion. What counts is not even our half-conscious, and therefore superficial, desire, but something deeper, more final and definitive. This is difficult to express in words.

Ignatius Loyola, with penetrating insight into essentials, regarded the will to will as the ultimate depth of human life. In this abyss, man is safely supported and unassailable, even though he may be in the greatest distress from misfortune and grief. Not even myself, not even my deepest despair, can extinguish the fundamental movement of the human will towards the positive: "If only things were different!" In this ultimate depth of his own self, man feels the pressure of reality and is irresistibly attached to it. One thing at least is infinitely more than he is: the will to will.

In the psalms, which are often simply songs of human sadness, this fundamental longing for God is presented as the innermost and central human reality. The fundamental note of the human soul is "How long, O Lord?" (Ps. 13, 1). "O God, thou art my God, I seek thee, my soul thirsts for thee . . ." (Ps. 63, 1–2). "I stretch out my hands to thee; my soul thirsts for thee like a parched land" (Ps. 143, 6). "My soul longs, yea, faints . . ." (Ps. 84, 2). The biblical image of the thirsty stag has impressed itself unforgettably on the memory of mankind. "As a hart longs for flowing streams, so longs my soul for thee, O God. My soul thirsts for God, for the living God. When shall I come and behold the face of God?" (Ps. 42, 1–3). Psalm 119 is a canticle of human longing: "With open mouth I pant" (v. 131); "My soul is consumed with longing" (v. 20); "At midnight I rise to praise thee" (v. 62); "My soul languishes for thy salvation" (v. 81).

As regards the second point, we must remember that the foundation of faith is not its demonstrability. If we are to give good counsel to people nowadays, and prevent their doubt from turning to despair, we must take their doubt seriously. Doubt shows how much lumber we carry around with our faith. Doubt entices us forward, wakens us, threatens our comfort. We must not ask for everything all at once of someone in doubt. It is enough if he affirms the essentials of his faith, if he can feel and is impressed by the purity and the honesty of Christ, if he admires the greatness of the life that Christ has made possible. It is not on the plane of formulatable proofs that the essential of faith is at stake. Perhaps the person in doubt has nothing to say against faith on the plane of his "fundamental intention." So much naïvety, lack of depth, unsatisfactory apologetics, hurried by-passing of reality can bar the doubter's way to assent, or to acceptance of particular laws of the Church. Yet at the deeper level he often recognizes the greatness of Christ and the significance of the Church.

This recognition does not of itself by any means determine, however, whether the fundamental core of faith, which is affirmed, will in fact find its appropriate expression in the system of dogmas, formulations, and laws. It is therefore possible to be a genuine Christian, to affirm the fundamental truth of Christianity, and yet to postpone assent in regard to many questions, even dogmatic ones. Despite indecision in detail, a human being can give a living, global assent to Christ and have the determined intention to follow to the end the way he pointed out. In doubt, assent should and may be deferred. Essentially, faith is an illumination, a spiritual breakthrough to reality. Uncertainty and provisional inability to assent are sometimes a genuine exercise of the will to believe. Faith is not necessarily linked with the deductions that can be drawn from it. People may hold fast to the fundamental truth of revelation and draw life from it, with only an imperfect grasp of its implications, and without being able yet to make it fully and concretely the truth they are consciously living.

Augustine describes the fundamental attitude of the man of good counsel in regard to a Christian who is in doubt and is unsure of his way. Those who do not know the sighs and tears that even the slightest knowledge of God costs may be angry with such a person, he says, and those who have never strayed themselves may be harsh, but for his part he cannot. He would rather collaborate in seeking what is equally unknown to both of them. Neither should be bold or conceited enough to think that he already possesses the full truth. "Permit me—I can surely ask this of you—to listen to you, so that I can speak with you."

Given confidence in the mercy of God, which embraces both the counsellor and the person in doubt, the light of faith sometimes shines out. The fundamental trust in Christ is there again, although perhaps many expressions are missing. But, after all, the will is a love, a hunger of the intellect, a longing, an aspiration. May people who experience this longing, intermittently perhaps but all the more intensely, not be banished by believers refusing to associate with them. Through the ministry of those whose role is to give good counsel, the Church ought to recognize them as its true members, or at least have compassion on them. For in a dark world the Church has a vast work of consolation to perform.

Comfort the Afflicted

When consolation is in question, we have to ask ourselves whether, and when, we have offered it with mere words instead of in person. Instead of helping people to life-giving truth, have we given them a well-meant lie? What are the true principles of Christian consolation, based on faith?

First of all, to be permitted to console is a grace. The help that the comforter gives an afflicted person is a consolation for himself also. "Blessed be the God and Father of our Lord Jesus Christ, the Father of mercies and God of all comfort, who comforts us in all our affliction, so that we may be able to comfort those who are in any affliction, with the comfort with which we ourselves are comforted by God" (2 Cor. 1, 3-4). The desolation of human existence consists chiefly in not having anyone to turn to. The Bible describes in terms of childlike simplicity the God of consolation whose representative we have to be for our brethren. "As one whom his mother comforts, so will I comfort you" (Is. 66, 13).

In this connection we must remember that a person without consolation can often no longer find any access to God. In that case we are their only comfort, however unsure. We are dealing in many cases with someone who is no longer able to pray. We will quote two examples, to avoid lengthy discussion and detailed analysis. They vividly describe the situation where both self and God are lost, beyond reach. Claudius, the fratricidal king in

147

Hamlet, falls on his knees in vain; he cannot pray. And in his fairy tale *The Snow Queen,* H. C. Andersen describes the cold, lost state of little Kay: "He wanted to say the Our Father, but all he could remember was his two-times table." The whole existence of some of the people to whom we want to offer the consolation of faith, is often one of utter frustration, conscious futility. Faith perseveres nevertheless and refuses to abandon to total solitude and final desolation someone who has been abandoned by all (and apparently even by God). In a remarkable interpretation of Herod's feast, Reinhold Schneider once drew attention to the temptation to leave people to their fate out of cowardice. "When Salome was dancing, there were many guests at table with Herod. All of them shared in the guilt, whatever their reason for being there, if they took pleasure in it or simply stayed out of fear or cowardice. The price paid for the feast was the head of God's herald. Let us examine our conscience, whether we were guests with Herod, whether he did not invite us. Our place is not here, but simply and solely in places where truth is silent, suffers, and dies. Where we should be is in the secret vault of human distress. But if our conscience accuses us of having been at Herod's feast, perhaps what life remains to us, if taken seriously and used to the utmost, will even now be sufficient for us to be able to leave the tyrant's company forever, with all our heart and soul."

The Christian is called upon to console those who are abandoned, to make the lonely share in his own comfort (2 Cor. 1, 7). He must not keep to himself the heartfelt consolation he has received in faith, but must hand it on abundantly (cf. 2 Cor. 7, 4) and protect the afflicted and downcast from harm (cf. 2 Cor. 7, 1–16). What use is it our being Christians if someone

148

THE SPIRIT OF HOPE

near us has to lament: "Insults have broken my heart, so that I am in despair. I looked for pity, but there was none; and for comforters, but I found none" (Ps. 69, 21). Considering all the consolation we have received from God, we are under an obligation to stand up for our brethren, giving them support or opposing those who threaten them. And if we are to perserve in this attitude, we shall often have to do without human recognition.

Suffer Injustice Patiently

The evangelists report Christ's patience in remaining silent. "And Pilate again asked him, 'Have you no answer to make? See how many charges they bring against you.' But Jesus made no further answer, so that Pilate wondered" (Mk. 15, 4–5). Accusations, insinuations, calumnies, because unanswered, recoiled on the speakers. Silence may often be the answer that truth gives. The shattering and perplexing fact that Christ, the living truth, was silent, was his victory. Speech does not always bear witness. It is strange to realize that right tends to be on the side of those who patiently keep silent. Our silence can also proclaim that truth is fundamentally not so much a proposition as a reality that can carry conviction even by its silence. The patience that Christ asks of us—and that sometimes seems too much to expect of us—requires the kind of strength and generosity that will not allow even justifiable anger to breed more injustice, and refuses to call on wrong to bear witness against wrong. The Christian who can parry the forces of destruction and seek a settlement is one who is clear-sighted without impatience, silent and serviceable. Quite likely no one will thank him for following Christ's

149

command to be a peacemaker. But God will eternally credit him
with it and forgive him much as a consequence.

Forgive Injuries

What does a genuinely forgiving attitude actually mean? A
person who has it certainly does not say: "You were weak. I
understand you. We will not think any more of your moment
of weakness." Christ never "excused" anything; he simply forgot
the whole injury. It was no longer there—no suppressed feeling
of injury which perhaps would survive in some dark corner of
the soul. To forgive in the Christian sense means to expunge
a brother's fault, not only from our memory, but also from our
very being. Not to act "as though nothing had happened," but
to bear witness that "nothing has happened." That is the kind
of forgiveness that Peter encountered in the eyes of Christ, a new
hope of being allowed to go on again. Peter went out to "weep
bitterly" for his sin, and this brought deliverance and a future
open to God.

Pray for the Living and the Dead

What does it mean to pray for the living and the dead? It
means to turn to someone who is there for everyone simultaneously, who spans every realm of reality and has mercy on all.
Prayer is a vital exchange between friends who feel their lot is
linked. No creature stands alone before God; each knows that
a fellow creature is there praying with him, openly and mani-
festly in God's presence. Consequently, the place where creatures

are ultimately and most profoundly present to one another is none other than God. The creature finds those it loves in God as the ground of its own self. A human being has no other access to the innermost reality of the beloved. Love for a human partner will not recognize any measure; it is itself the measure of all things. That is why it is dependent on God. The very fact that human love is comprised in God's knowledge means prayer. With the gaze fixed on God, our finite affection becomes absolute surrender, love. Can any word of love ever be lost? "Immediately the father of the child cried out with tears and said, 'I believe; help my unbelief!'" (Mk. 9, 24). Such tears are perhaps the only thing that God cannot forget: "Thou my God hast put my tears in thy bottle" (Ps. 56, 9).

The "goodness and loving kindness (φιλανθρωπία) of God has appeared among us" (Tit. 3, 4). This breadth of heart is a revelation of God's own nature. What future has this God prepared for us, what path to happiness and selfhood has he opened out? Man cannot measure God's grace by his own heart. Throughout the history of salvation, from end to end of the Bible and in all the events of our own life, we can see that God's love for us is unchangeable, cannot be discouraged. But it is also true that a God of mere law and commandments would not be as "zealous" and "jealous" as a God of love.

8

The Future of Hope

When a Catholic theologian speaks about death, he inevitably also thinks of the events that represent an absolute limit set to self-development in this world, and that he calls the "last things." Usually he distinguishes eight of these: death, the particular judgment, heaven, hell, the resurrection of the body, the general judgment, Christ's second coming, and the transformation of the universe. We shall try to indicate the intrinsic connection of the items on this rather unsystematic list, while endeavoring to free them from some of the usual representations with which they have become interwoven, and so get to the essentials of Christian teaching about death. In questions of eschatology, Christian thought in recent times has undergone a change of perspectives. New and partly unaccustomed conceptions have been put forward and hypotheses framed which amount to a recasting of our previous representations. This is also the reason why our meditations cannot attempt even to outline an exhaustive and systematically elaborated treatise on the events of the last days.

Antitheses in Faith

The first thing we have to note is that the Christian learns from revelation that there can be different and to some extent opposed attitudes towards death.

Death Is Both Meaningful and Meaningless

For the Christian, death is not a meaningless end or a final collapse, but the transition to a world that he has always longed for, a world of fulfillment. Christ taught his disciples: "Do not fear those who [only] kill the body but cannot kill the soul" (Mt. 10, 28). Surely this "only" is a mockery? Surely Christ himself was deeply affected by the death of his friend Lazarus? John makes us feel Christ's emotion. He shows that Christ "was deeply moved in spirit," that he felt anger at the grief and the destructive power of death. On the way to the grave he felt revulsion against its stroke: "When Jesus saw her [Mary] weeping, and the Jews who came with her also weeping, he was deeply moved in spirit and troubled" (Jn. 11, 33–34), that is, he gave himself up to the emotion he felt. Finally, intense grief burst out from Christ's soul. He cried out "with a loud voice" the words of life into the tomb (Jn. 11, 43).

Death Is Both Punishment and Promise

Despite a fundamental change in the conception of evolution, the majority of theologians still continue to regard the sin of the so-called first human pair as decisive for our psychosomatic fallen

153

state. They teach that the original ancestors of the human race committed a grave sin by transgressing the command imposed on them as a test, and so incurred eternal damnation. The sin of the first parents then passed to all their descendants and was the cause of guilt of a special kind in them. The reason why the guilty condition is inherited is said to be the natural genetic link with the first parents of mankind.

Irenaeus of Lyons, on the other hand, regarded our condition of fragility caused by original sin as an expression of God's universal saving will. According to him and other Fathers of the Church, the expulsion of man from Paradise may be considered an act by which God turned in mercy to men. He teaches that God banished man from the tree of life out of mercy, so that he should not remain a sinner forever and so that sin should not be immortal, or evil without remedy. God therefore set a limit to transgression by creating death, and made an end to sin by the dissolution of the flesh, so that man might cease to live in sin and by dying might begin to exist for God. This is an approach that has not yet been followed up by theology even today.

Man Is Both Mortal and Immortal

We shall first quote without comment a passage from Karl Barth. "The word 'immortality' does not occur at all in the Old Testament, and only twice in the New. That fact alone is noteworthy. But the sense in which it is used on these two occasions is even more so. It is said (1 Tim. 6, 16) not that man, but that God has immortality, and indeed that he, who alone is Sovereign, alone has immortality. The meaning clearly is that man has not, either man as a whole, or in part of himself. He has not immortality from the start, nor can he obtain it for himself in some way. Immortality could only come to man (each man) as something new and unmerited, as a free gift from him who alone possesses it, and who alone is immortal by his very essence. The other relevant passage (1 Cor. 15, 53) speaks of this. It speaks of the resurrection of the dead as a new free act of God for all men, in virtue of which mortal will put on immortality as a garment. We must face the fact that man in himself and as such, with all that he is and does, is, according to the testimony of the Bible, mortal, that is, he is not immortal at all."

On the other hand, we should like to raise on principle the question of how human corporeality is to be understood, what place it has in the universe, for what hope it was created. The important insight that man with body and soul occupies a central position in the universe is unquestionable. The human body is the locus of man's most radical link with the universe, the hinge (*caro-cardo*) of the world. In our body, matter is united with spirit. The nature of spirit consists in being infinitely open to the infinite. This means that in man's body the world becomes open to God, and thereby comes into the presence of the Absolute. According to Christian philosophy, man is not composed of two "things" (matter and spirit) but is a single being; the two give rise to a third which is identical with neither of them. The human body is the explication of the soul. Conversely, the human soul is the highest actuation of the human body. When we say, as we are accustomed to, that the human soul is spiritual, independent of matter, that is only a partial truth. Certainly the human soul is spirit, but the latter enters into matter with a necessity that belongs to its very nature. It becomes soul precisely by its union with matter. In view of these considerations, we should have to say that the soul "gathers" from the universe the matter which, under the influence of the spirit, becomes the body.

Both lines of thought—man's mortality and his orientation

towards immortality—find their answer in Christ's resurrection. After completing his work of redemption, the Son of God did not lay aside his human body, did not become "pure spirit." His human face remains forever the face of God. In the risen Christ the human body entered into the life of the blessed Trinity.

Christ the Summit of All Cosmic Dynamism

The universe evolves from its original state of being in the direction of life. Life is perfected in the human spirit. Christ raises this spirit to the perfection of immortality. Consequently, Christ is man in his ultimate state, the summit of the whole cosmic dynamism. He draws all the forces of the universe to himself, and forwards, and ever higher into the realm of perfect fulfillment. Fundamentally, he became man so that he might lead our mortal life to immortality. Christ is the predestined world. The dynamism of the universe narrows and is concentrated in the course of thousands of millions of years into this single focal point of reference, the incarnate Logos. This total evolution converging in the historical Christ then presses forwards over the whole breadth of the cosmos and history to include all reality.

Death as Final Decision

We usually think of human death as the separation of the soul from the body. Is such a separation possible, in view of what has just been said? When brought before the council in Jerusalem, Paul said something very important for our interpretation of human death: ". . . with respect to the hope and the resurrection of the dead I am on trial" (Acts 23, 6). The affirmation that death was conquered in Christ's resurrection is central in the Christian message. Since then, what happens in man's death is not an absolute frontier of life. We should like briefly to summarize here our own view, which we have already expounded elsewhere. "In death the possibility of man's first fully personal decision opens out. Consequently, death is the place where man attains full awareness, where he meets God and decides his eternal lot."

In order to show the full import of this hypothesis, we must first give the reasons that lead us to think of human death in this hopeful way. Our hypothesis suggests that only at the moment of death can man set aside the alien character that affects him; only in death does he become ontologically capable of full encounter with God (in Christ) and of making a definitive decision about him. Every human being, therefore, would have the opportunity in death to decide in regard to Christ with complete clarity. On this basis we should like to think out afresh the theology of death.

Grounds for This Hypothesis Concerning Death

Even our finest experiences of God in this life are superficial. Our relation to God is unreal, uncertain, and fleeting, a momentary encounter in passing. Every human being lives on the surface, precisely because he is human. A strange incapacity dominates our inner life; we cannot see and do the one thing necessary. How is a transfigured world to arise from this fragmented life? We shall attempt by a brief analysis of human action to show man's "ontological incapacity."

Man Is Incapable of Full Awareness of the Scope of His Own Desire

His will is split between the limitlessness of aspiration and the limits set to realization. With inexorable necessity, man desires something more, something unattained. Something mysterious animates him, perpetually driving his actions forward to new goals and promises. In every single action man aims into infinity, even though the concrete goal he wants to attain is always something finite. However much the will may have attained by its own power, achievement never corresponds to the secret desire that prompted it.

All this means that man has within him a dynamism towards what is humanly unattainable, towards the Absolute. This tension is hard to bear. A life that is reaching for the Absolute and at the same time is cramped and hemmed in, is extremely burdensome. As a result, people only too often attempt to take the provisional for the final. But even so they remain unhappy and unsatisfied, though perhaps without admitting it. Human life could only find fulfillment, or, rather, man would only really come to birth as a human being, if human longing, the drive towards the unattainable, were suddenly to find itself faced with its true object; if the Absolute, the unattainable, were there in front of him, radiant and concretely experienced. That would be the moment of his real birth as a human being. Fully free and personal meeting with Christ is stamped into the very structure of human aspiration. This characteristic of human existence is

158

even more evident in the mysterious process which we call cognition.

Cognition Orientates Man Dynamically Towards the Absolute

In cognition, the mind takes some tangible reality into itself. By this intussusception of the various individual objects of the world, man begins to become familiar with his surroundings. He gradually comes to understand how things, living creatures, and human beings behave. But all that is merely detailed factual knowledge. Man perpetually endeavors to compose these fragments of knowledge into a system and to a large extent fails to do so. He thus discovers that he has a vague adumbration of something greater and more comprehensive, something that cannot be built up out of his items of knowledge. This makes him realize that his urge to know is infinitely more than mere curiosity. From the start, his mind has been drawn by an absolute, by the plenitude of reality.

On the one hand, therefore, man only knows what is limited; at the same time, however, or rather, even before, he strives above and beyond it into the limitless, to what has no limits set to its being. In every concrete act of knowing, the wholly Other is co-known and co-desired. This transcendence of the mind towards the wholly Other, which can never be explicitly and directly grasped in consciousness, is the ground that makes possible all other cognitive activity. In the sphere of his cognition, torn between limited and unlimited, man would reach fulfillment only if the Absolute were to become a reality that he could concretely grasp. In every act of cognition, man aspires to this inconceivable event, a meeting with the infinite which has become finite, with Christ. This paradoxical character of human existence appears even more clearly in the course of human love.

Human Love Transcends All Realization

Two persons who love each other bring about a real union by the "We" that they utter and constitute by what they are. Love consists in a real exchange, whereby two human beings live in a relationship that is entirely mutual. The reality of the one becomes the ground of the other's reality, by mutual gift. This at once indicates an ultimate element in human love. What is really intended in love transcends any actual realization. Love involves an aspiration reaching out towards the totality of being, because love unrestrictedly affirms a being who is limited. Consequently, what love seeks is essentially more than anything that can in fact be effectively attained.

A created being, finite and fragile, becomes by our love the object of our aspiration towards the infinite. To be the object of another human being's love is, therefore, an exacting demand which no one can adequately meet. Human love cannot be humanly fulfilled. An absolute is always implied and sought in it, if it is lived seriously, maturely, and honestly. Such love could only be perfectly fulfilled if the absolute and infinite were to be represented with perfect clarity, in a finite human being, as lovable because loving the free affirmation of reality.

Let us sum up this inchoative outline analysis of human aspiration, cognition, and love. The central significance of all these human activities includes a clear, free, total personal encounter with Christ, with the unconditional that has become conditioned, as the "Omega point," the condition of the possibility of complete human realization. Only when this actually happens does man truly become man.

It is clear that even this brief sketch of the structure of human reality already includes an important statement about death, and that this confirms the hypothesis formulated at the beginning regarding a final decision in death. Only in death does a human being become fully a person, and only then can he definitively attain his salvation by freely shaping his own being in view of Christ. We shall confirm this conclusion by two considerations, one negative, the other positive.

Only in Death Does a Human Being Become Fully a Person

1. MAN'S INNER DISPERSION

Man has not chosen his concrete circumstances just as they are, but received them, with all their advantages and disadvantages, from his parents and family circle, from the cultural climate of his social milieu, from the stage of development of mankind, and even from man's origins in pre-human forms of life.

In this way an alien material has gradually accumulated, out of which man has to shape himself into a person. This alien web of circumstance produced, elaborated, and co-determined by others, intrinsically restricts him. During his life on earth he strives to enable his genuine, innermost, yet still unknown self to emerge. He is working, however, on an already formed, ready-made material, his predetermined situation in the world. He is never able totally to overcome the strangeness and opacity of his own factual circumstances.

The first possibility of being what he inwardly aspires to be yet cannot be will come within his grasp only when he lays aside his restricted, alien circumstances and receives, and indeed makes for himself, a new expression of his being freely determined according to his own mind, that is to say, in death.

His superficial factual circumstances also involve temporal limitation. Dispersed in his very essence, man cannot dominate the succession of temporal moments. He enters into reality only one moment at a time. The particular present, the extent of time that is his, is not sufficient for him to achieve the full wealth that is in him. His life cannot unfold into an undivided present. It is not in his power to live the moment in its fullness. It is not possible to say that he "is" in the true sense of the term; he merely "ex-sists," lives all the time outside himself. Only at the moment when he no longer moves on into the same fragmented future can he live his interior reality in an undivided present. But that moment can only come in death. It is only then that there is no further advance into indeterminate open future.

2. MAN'S SELF-REALIZATION AS MAN

Let us imagine a human life that has developed fully from birth to death in accordance with its inherent dynamism. What would have taken place in such an existence? Two lines of life can be discerned in it. At the intersection of the two is what happens in death.

The "outer man." This expression does not here simply stand for the body, but denotes the whole human being to the extent that his entire existence, body and soul, is directed outwards towards externals. What are these external things? In the first place, a growth of the biological powers, a development and growth to maturity of the organism, a progressive differentiation and specialization of the various faculties (growth in knowl-

162

edge, broadening of the intellectual horizons, awakening to freedom, friendship, and love). Man "conquers" the world in its
various dimensions, the world of things, of knowledge, of personal relationships.

But as man throws himself into this secular business, external
things begin to consume his personal existence. Even in his task
of mastering the world, man visibly fails. He becomes aware
of the poverty of human existence. He realizes how many chances
in life he has missed. Everywhere he is conscious of limits.
Everything turns into the treadmill of daily routine, with all its
duties, fatigues, and disappointments. With terrible clarity he
realizes that he has failed in essentials, in honesty, friendship,
humility, love. Life loses its freshness, its verve, its novelty. The
outer man is worn out—a fate that no one can escape.

The "inner man." But is this the whole of human life? Precisely
by coming to realize his own limits, in the crises of personal life,
in the exhaustion of the outer man, something is built up which
could be designated by the word "person." The energies of the
outer man are transformed into an interior reality. The mature
human being comes into existence, something hidden, an existence which despite its narrow limits can grow into the infinite.
Out of his externals man gathers together an interior. He becomes a center of reality. Precisely by permitting his life to be
worn out by the events of every day, authentic life has come to
birth in him.

If we extend the lines of this dialectic and draw the final
conclusion from it, the following picture of death emerges. In
death, by the total loss of everything external, total interiority is
attained. In death alone, therefore, man becomes wholly himself,
definitively a person, an absolutely independent center of being.

In death man finally becomes adult: free, aware, and uncon-
fined; capable of making a final decision. In this decision he
lives the clearest meeting with Christ of his life.

Consequences that Follow from This Hypothesis about Death

If the individual *eschata* are regarded in this perspective, consequences follow which oblige the theologian to undertake a fresh
examination of some of his own ideas.

The True Human Being Comes to Be by Resurrection

The word "resurrection" here stands as a cipher, that is to say,
as a symbol of what cannot be stated, as an explanation of the
inexplicable. Resurrection means existential completeness, direct
relation in soul and body with the universe. Corporeality unfolds
into personal being. Man posits his own eternity in his final
decision. Immortality becomes a total personal event of man as
a soul-body unity and therefore as resurrection. In this perspective there is no longer any difference between immortality and
resurrection. From this it is clear that:

The Resurrection Must Be Universal

The universe is concentrated in man. We are children of the
earth, which is not merely the scene of our separate, independent
self-development, but belongs to our essential constitution. If
immortality happens with our soul, then this must be called

resurrection; if it happens with our body, then this must also mean transfiguration of the universe. It follows that:

The Universe Must Be Judged

The expression arouses an unpleasant feeling in us. However, the more one considers the world, its motives, its struggle for power and self-assertion, the more one realizes that we do not yet live in a world as it ought to be. The world must be judged and righted—not condemned, but set right. The world is only as it by rights should be if the good is beautiful, the truth good, and being radiant. Such a world does not yet exist. It is established by us through our personal decision in death.

The Judgment Is Also Purification

On this hypothesis the fire of purgatory can be thought of as the quality and intensity of the decision for God taking place in death. In a single moment, love for God floods man, who must then rise to God with his uttermost strength. Individual human beings would therefore in a single moment, in death, undergo a personal process of purification different in each.

Christ Is Still in Process of Becoming

Christ appears in his full cosmic growth when all human beings who are to constitute his "plenitude" (pleroma) have encountered him with the love that creates real union.

The Meaning of Life Consists in Active Preparation for Death

Man must try during his life to arrive at that resoluteness in personal life that will enable him to make the right decision in death. The literature of Christian sprituality calls this attitude "vigilance" in regard to salvation. The idea of a final possibility of decision does not lessen in any way our vigilant concern about salvation. When the need for it is seen to follow ineluctably from the clearly understood situation that we move forwards towards a final decision in death, its necessity is more far-reaching and demanding than any morality of mere commands and prohibitions, of mere prescriptions and orders imposed from outside on our personal life. It follows from the essential constitution of man. You have only one life, so you simply must succeed with it.

The Meaning of Life Consists in the Exercise of Virtue

Virtue is the fulfillment of human capacity for reality, a lasting orientation towards essentials. It means essential human quality realized through personal effort and lived as testimony. It is the deep current of a destiny successfully achieved.

Spiritual Deepening of the Hypothesis Regarding Death

The attitude just described is threatened during our lifetime, not so much by individual acts of rebellion as by an imperceptible drift into inauthenticity, which for our purpose we might tentatively call a sinful way of living life itself. There is such a thing as a life which is forfeit through misuse.

This sinful way of living life has nothing dramatic or Promethean about it. Impatience, petty egotism in everyday affairs, lack of respect for other human beings and their own lives, spite, rash judgment, smugness—all that and much else would have to be considered when speaking of that sin.

At what points is this threat to our life particularly concentrated? What is the source of that obscuration of reality which shuts out Christ's influence, closes the soul to God?

The most important New Testament text for the analysis of the kind of sin we are trying to describe is the account of Christ's temptations in St. Matthew's Gospel (Mt. 4, 1–11). This gives three points that can serve as basis for an outline account of the essential temptation to which human life is exposed.

Success

Impelled by the Spirit, Christ leaves human security behind. He has reached an extremity: "And he fasted forty days and forty nights." Then the tremendous temptation befalls him. What if he were to change stones into bread? What was the point of this temptation? To persuade Christ to externalize that power which was present in the depth of his humanity. But with the concentrated force of his theandric existence, by his rejection of the tempter, Christ entered on the venture of living from within, of standing among the oppressed and the downtrodden, of enduring the poverty and powerlessness of being human. He would be interior disposition only, a life of inner truth and experience, falling and dying into the earth for others. A new future and world order for mankind was thus made possible. A man is more than his success.

Thirst for Power

A dizzy attraction seized Christ's soul. In spirit he stood on the pinnacle of the temple, saw the vertiginous fall, the abyss, and swarming crowds. The Messiah must be extraordinary, exercise his power over the soul and heart of man. The tempter wanted to contrive to get God's incarnation revealed by a bold show of force and so be essentially misunderstood. At that moment, Christ gazed deep into our souls, and saw that only a humble man can approach human suffering. His dazzling glory would destroy us.

Wealth

What was the meaning of the temptation when Christ was taken up on a high mountain, saw all the kingdoms of the world and their glory and when the tempter said to him: "All these I will give you if you will fall down and worship me"? What disturbance was this in the soul of the God-man? The whole world lay at his feet. Nevertheless, Christ rejected precisely this feeling as a temptation. He went down from this exalted height of feeling into the triviality of ordinary existence. In the world of the poor he wanted to bear witness to unconditional initiative, patience, and accomplishment: interior detachment from things, self-conquest, silence, spiritual poverty. That was the mode of life Christ chose for himself. He wanted to be exposed to the immediate impact of the moment and the human need and distress which it manifests. He wanted recognition of the personal life of others, creative presence. The attitude of spiritual poverty characterizes people who have attained interior freedom; they may even possess this world's goods, but if so, they are not possessed by them. Inner freedom permits truly personal relations with others.

The "Fire of Purgatory" as Putting on the Mind of Christ

In death, a similar sort of decision is made. All the existential inauthenticity that a human being has amassed within him collapses. Man is confronted with what he really is, with what has eternal significance. His success is destroyed, his power evaporates, his wealth disappears. Nothing external supports him. What is left when a human being abandons himself completely? He recognizes then that all that ever endured in life was what he had given up: selflessness. The moments of unselfishness come together to form his true reality, the hours of endurance with a suffering friend, the experiences of loving devotion, the will to mourn with those who mourn, to rejoice with those who rejoice, to share others' human concerns.

This reduction of man to his essential disposition is simply purgatory. It is man's meeting with what he is, the concentration of his whole life, a momentary occurrence of self-realization in the abyss of death. But man cannot be completely himself in this way without at the same time becoming aware, by his own attainment of humanity, of the reality of the Word made man. Man's meeting with himself therefore becomes a meeting with God through Christ. This is not a supplementary dimension in the process of death; it is the revelation of the grace-given incorporation of human reality into that of Christ. By meeting himself with complete honesty, man meets Christ.

Self-Realization as Judgment

St. Matthew's Gospel (25, 31ff.) transmits one of Jesus' sayings where the righteous (and also the unrighteous) ask Christ: "Lord, when did we do that? When did we see you hungry or thirsty or a stranger or naked or sick or in prison?" They had accomplished the greatest actions of their lives without realizing what they were doing.

On the basis of these words of Christ, provided their sense is not minimized, and the concept of the judgment which Christ himself expresses in these words, it would be possible to frame a theology of encounter with Christ. This encounter takes place in the hidden center of our personal life. The judgment will manifest that dimension of our actions which is directly linked with Christ, whatever their transitory concrete empirical character. The ultimate ground of our experiences, hope, aspirations, desire for friendship, kindness, and human relationships, and of course our unpretentious actions of unselfish help, is Jesus Christ himself.

Christ Lives in the Depths of All Things (The "Descent into Hell")

An important task of a present-day Christology would be to work out a theology of this Christ dimension of our existence and show its importance in our spiritual life. Here we shall

draw attention to only one aspect of it, which is often over-
looked in preaching: Christ's "descent into hell." Christ has
entered into the depth of the world. He went down into the
deep background stratum of reality which radically unifies it
all. What is referred to is the deep and innermost center of the
universe, not only in the cosmic sense but also in the historical,
personal, and existential orders.

By going down to the ground of the world by his death—
continuing the descent made in his incarnation—into the "heart
of the earth" (as St. Matthew's Gospel tells us), he became
present to the whole of pre-Christian mankind. The universe
is no longer the same as before, for Christ himself lives in its
depths, in its essence and ground. Christ has become the mysterious center of all created change and development. From now
on, every death, every dying into the world, is an entry into
Christ, and each act of dying—which in the concrete means
every unselfish, humanly helpful action or exultation felt at
something great—is itself faith, salvation, relationship with Christ.
By becoming the depth of the world, Christ has transformed
the situation in regard to salvation. In the depth of all that is
humanly valid, Christ is met with. A world restored is in the
making; heaven is growing.

In this view, the judgment is a revelation of the essence of
things and of the disposition of the human heart and, consequently, a meeting with the ground of grounds, Jesus Christ.
But if the judgment is not to be viewed so abstractly as to be
completely unreal, we must allow our heart to help us understand what all this means. The human being will suddenly be
faced with what is eternally valid in him, and discover that his
feelings and impulses have formed part of what Christ is, have
shared in those of God's own heart. In the depths of all his

dreams and aspirations there was always a single factor—Christ. Nothing else counts, everything else falls away, no longer presents any obstacle, or prevents man from entering into perfect joy. The judgment is a message of joy.

Can God Damn Anyone?

Hell is not something that simply happens from outside; it is not something that God imposes on us afterwards for our misdeeds. It is not a great culmination, ardent, asphyxiating. It is simply a human being who is totally identified with what he is, with what he can forcibly acquire and accomplish of himself. It is the mode of existence of a human being who is satisfied in himself, for all eternity; he has nothing more and desires nothing more than himself. Hell is not a threat; it is the ontological projection of our own pettiness. There is no tragic grandeur about hell, because fundamentally there cannot be any "place" which is hell. There is only a state of heart. Everything lives in heaven, because God created the world in view of heaven. And heaven is experienced through a state of heart. Those who have become poor can appreciate its beauty. Those who have remained rich must be content with their own wealth. Those who can endure heaven (who can lovingly receive more and so give more) are in heaven, live in the eternal happiness of being able to love, of no longer belonging to themselves, of no longer having to possess themselves. The only people who cannot endure heaven are those who no longer find it in them to love.

Sin, the fire of purgatory, judgment, and hell: we have medi-

tated on these terrible words only to conclude in the end that
the only word that has eternal validity is love.

Heaven as the Essence of Our Future

What do we arrive at if we project our deepest experience of the
life and vitality of the world into heaven? We think of a world
of full growth and expansion, lived in God's company, inte-
grating the whole process of evolution, all life and feeling that
exists in the world—from inorganic matter through organisms
to spirit—into the infinite happiness of God.

Revelation adds one image after another to suggest to us
plainly and simply a boundless happiness eternally bestowed:
I shall be a God to him, and he shall be my child; the just will
sit with Christ on the throne of God; they will judge the world,
they will shine like the sun; God will give them the morning
star. These are all images of happiness, purity, clarity, and vitality; intelligible to the simplest, and yet by their profound svm-
bolism they transcend everything that can be expressed. What
theologian has yet fully drawn out the wealth contained in these
metaphors of sitting on God's throne, judging the world, being
sun and light, bearing a crown of glory, possessing the morning
star?

What does Christ promise? To a Samaritan woman, water;
to the people, bread; to fishermen, nets filled to overflowing; to
merchants, precious pearls; to the farm-worker that his hoe will
one day unexpectedly unearth a treasure; to the peasants, an
abundant harvest; to us all, knowledge and security. The Book
of Revelation is radiant with all the colors in the world; precious

stones gleam; the voices of nature accompany men's songs of triumph; the air is filled with perfumes rising from golden vessels. He who is true and faithful comes on a white horse accompanied by squadrons of horsemen. His name is Word of God, King of Kings. His mantle is soaked in blood. In a final battle he saved our nature for fulfillment. He is celebrating the marriage feast of the Lamb. A voice rings out from heaven: "He who conquers, I will make him a pillar in the temple of my God; never shall he go out of it." To be a pillar in God's temple means to be continually active, to bear up the world, secure and serene, in the eternal vitality of unending personal life.

Jesus repeatedly describes eternal life as union with God. "If a man loves me, he will keep my word, and my Father will love him, and we will come to him and make our home with him." "You will eat and drink at my table in my kingdom." "Behold, I stand at the door and knock; if any one hears my voice and opens the door, I will come in to him and eat with him, and he with me. He who conquers, I will grant him to sit with me on my throne, as I myself conquered and sat down with my Father on his throne." God becomes my beloved, forever.

Let us now try to forget the words and catch some glimpse of the mysterious import of Christ's prayer at the Last Supper: "Father, the world has not known thee, but I have known thee; and these know that thou hast sent me. I made known to them thy name, and I will make it known, that the love with which thou hast loved me may be in them and I in them."

This love of God in us will unfold in heaven into an eternal reality. One hardly dares try to express what that means in growing intensity of being and radiant personal life. It is ultimately of little importance whether we are immortal by nature, or in what form the world will awaken in us to the new being of the resurrection. We love God; God loves us. His love is infinite and embraces all that is. That love will become our own being, experienced, accomplished, and eternal.

Testimony of Joy

Christ's resurrection has inaugurated the last days. To remain true to our vocation to love God, we must live here and now as though we were already in heaven. That is our destiny and our mission. Under various names God incarnate promised us life: kingdom of heaven, land of the living, perfect consolation, fulfillment of our desires, boundless mercy, the company of God. He also pointed out our way to this: detachment from self, gentleness, peacemaking, hunger and thirst for "righteousness." All these are essential characteristics of the love by which man receives himself by giving himself.

This brings us to the end of our meditations on the future of earthly reality. All our reflections have led in the end to God's joy. The Christian should carry this silent, unobtrusive joy out into a world that knows so little joy and so much sorrow.